CW01310077

The POWER of SPEAKING

How to Become Confident and Assertive

YOUR TRUTH

HARINDER GHATORA

BALBOA PRESS
A DIVISION OF HAY HOUSE

Copyright © 2019 Harinder Ghatora.

Image credits: Shutterstock

All rights reserved. No part of this book may be used or reproduced by any means, graphic, electronic, or mechanical, including photocopying, recording, taping or by any information storage retrieval system without the written permission of the author except in the case of brief quotations embodied in critical articles and reviews.

Balboa Press books may be ordered through booksellers or by contacting:

Balboa Press
A Division of Hay House
1663 Liberty Drive
Bloomington, IN 47403
www.balboapress.com
1 (877) 407-4847

Because of the dynamic nature of the Internet, any web addresses or links contained in this book may have changed since publication and may no longer be valid. The views expressed in this work are solely those of the author and do not necessarily reflect the views of the publisher, and the publisher hereby disclaims any responsibility for them.

The author of this book does not dispense medical advice or prescribe the use of any technique as a form of treatment for physical, emotional, or medical problems without the advice of a physician, either directly or indirectly. The intent of the author is only to offer information of a general nature to help you in your quest for emotional and spiritual well-being. In the event you use any of the information in this book for yourself, which is your constitutional right, the author and the publisher assume no responsibility for your actions.

Any people depicted in stock imagery provided by Getty Images are models, and such images are being used for illustrative purposes only. Certain stock imagery © Getty Images.

Print information available on the last page.

ISBN: 978-1-9822-2465-3 (sc)
ISBN: 978-1-9822-2467-7 (hc)
ISBN: 978-1-9822-2466-0 (e)

Library of Congress Control Number: 2019903701

Balboa Press rev. date: 04/10/2019

I dedicate this book to all the wonderful people I have had the pleasure of working with in my private practice. I hope this book helps you to find your voice.

On this day of your life,
Harinder, I believe God wants you to know
that you may speak your truth but soothe your words with peace.

Tell your truth as soon as you know it. Yet tell it gently,
kindly, and with compassion for the hearer. Someone
needs to hear the truth from you today, but that person
also needs your deep compassion as you speak it.

Seek to say what needs to be said with softness, and with
a wide-open heart. Remember, the truth can hurt—but it
hurts a lot less if you care how it feels while saying it.

Love,

Your friend
Neale

—Neale Donald Walsch
Author of *Conversations with God*
http://www.nealedonaldwalsch.com

Contents

Acknowledgements xi
Introduction xiii

Chapter 1   Understanding What Speaking Your Truth
             Really Means 1
Chapter 2   The Origins of your Passive Behaviour 9
Chapter 3   Why Speaking Your Truth Matters 18
Chapter 4   What You Stand to Gain by Speaking Your Truth ... 29
Chapter 5   Why You Are Afraid to Speak Up 34
Chapter 6   Overcoming Your Fears and Changing Your
             Unhealthy Beliefs 54
Chapter 7   A Road Map for Creating Change in Your Life 85
Chapter 8   How to Internalize Your New-Found Beliefs 106
Chapter 9   Additional Sources of Help on your
             Assertiveness Journey 122
Chapter 10   Assertiveness in Action 149
Chapter 11   Your Assertiveness Action Plan 175

About the Author 189

Acknowledgements

I am deeply grateful to my soul sister and editor, Harminder Sehmi of Harmony Writing and Editing Services, for her invaluable contribution to shaping and refining this book. Had it not been for her expertise, knowledge, and loving contribution, this book would simply not have come to fruition in the form that it has.

I would also like to thank my dear friend Sukhi Bhogal of Sukhi Solutions, who carried out the research for the chapter on alternative therapies. She always has been, and I've no doubt will continue to be, a source of endless and inspiring knowledge.

I owe a debt of gratitude to all my counselling and coaching clients, for it is they who inspired me to write this book in the first place.

I am thankful to Neale Donald Walsch for granting me permission to use the epigraph.

I am also grateful to the staff at Balboa Press for their guidance, expertise and support throughout the publishing process.

And, finally, I am eternally grateful to my family: my mum, my dad, my husband and two amazing children. Your encouragement and support kept me focused throughout the long process of writing this book. Thank you. You are the foundation of my entire existence and will probably never fully know how precious you are to me.

Introduction

I remember it as if it were yesterday—the nauseating feeling I had seconds after agreeing to attend a work training event that would take me away from my eight-month-old son for a whole weekend. My stomach muscles tensed up. I felt hot and clammy. I was overcome with anxiety. The internal conflict was debilitating. I absolutely did not want to go. How could I possibly leave my baby for all that time? We had never been apart for more than a few hours. I knew I didn't want to go, but why couldn't I say no?

I distinctly remember my feelings of disgust on another occasion, when I found myself listening to an acquaintance making outrageously crude and derogatory remarks about a young lady he'd met up with. I sat there politely smiling when what I really wanted to do was challenge not only the validity of what he was saying but also the disrespectful way in which he was saying it. But I couldn't bring myself to say anything. I couldn't even show my repulsion by getting up and walking away. I felt sick with frustration. I was deeply disappointed in myself for not being able to speak my truth.

Since you've picked up this book, I'm guessing you've been there too, like so many of us. And you know exactly how it feels: that moment when someone in your life—a relative, co-worker, acquaintance, or even a stranger—expresses a view you vehemently disagree with. You know what it's like to feel the tension, the irritation, and perhaps even the anger rising deep inside—the energy surging upwards, seeking some sort of verbal expression. You desperately want to put that person straight, to correct him or her, to tell the person that he or she is wrong. But you can't. The words just won't come out. So you stand there, silent. Something stops you from opening your mouth. Something stops you from finding your voice. Something stops you from speaking your truth. And this happens again and again and again.

This situation and these feelings were once very familiar to me. I lived most of my young adult life in this way, never saying what I really wanted to say. I would outwardly agree with everyone around me, but inwardly I would be vehemently disagreeing; outwardly I would be nice and polite, but inwardly I would struggle to control my emotional reactions to what others were saying or doing. On some occasions, the internal conflict was on an epic scale.

I would find phrases like "Sure, no problem …"; "No, it's fine …"; and "Yes, of course …" coming out of my mouth in an instant— way before I had even given a second thought to what was being asked of me. More often than not, these phrases would be responses to situations that clearly were a problem, were not fine at all, and needed a "Sorry, but I can't do that …" response.

I'm pleased to say that these experiences are now firmly in my past. I no longer choose to live my life in such a timid, compliant, and people-pleasing way. Over the years, I've learnt to kindly, politely, but firmly state my truth. I still commonly say, "Sure, no problem …" and "No, it's fine …" and "Yes, of course …" But now these phrases come after a moment of true inner reflection on the situation in hand and my ability and willingness to comply. I can truly say that this is a far more healthy and harmonious way to live compared with the internal warfare that was previously raging inside me. To reach this place, I had to go on a deep inner journey. In this book, I would like to take you on this same journey of self-discovery and positive change.

I'm a qualified and experienced counsellor and holistic life coach and have worked with hundreds of people in my private practice. Over the years, I've noticed that a common cause of direct and indirect unhappiness in many of my clients' lives is their tendency to not speak their truth. When you are unable to communicate your wishes and needs to those around you in a clear, firm, but polite way, it often means that at best your needs are unmet, and at worst you are misunderstood, ignored, or simply walked all over. Over many years, the internal tension that can build up has the potential to cause you serious mental and physical harm. It has the potential to warp your personality and wreck your relationships.

I chose to write this book for two reasons. Firstly, I believe that the simple practice of speaking your truth sits right at the heart of a happy, balanced and fulfilled life. As human beings, we are all permanently in relationship firstly with ourselves, secondly with those around us, and thirdly with our environment. For every one of us, there is only ever one person at the centre of our universe—ourselves. If we want to make meaningful connections with others, have closeness in our relationships, live a satisfying life, and have a strong, healthy, respectful sense of self, then we must learn to identify and communicate what we truly feel, need, and expect from others.

The second reason is that through my client work I have realized that many people are conditioned to believe that there are only two modes of expression: a passive, quiet, compliant way or a loud, angry, aggressive way. It is this "either/or" perception that I wish to challenge. There is another way—the middle way. My aim in writing this book is to present and promote this middle way, in which you speak your truth firmly but gently and kindly. This is the assertive way.

I am honoured that you have chosen to engage with this book and embark on this journey of self-discovery and learning. Together we are going to look at

- what it means to speak your truth—and some common misconceptions that people have;
- how and why you learnt to not speak your truth;
- the mental, emotional, and physical consequences of not speaking your truth;
- the underlying thought patterns and beliefs that prevent you from expressing yourself fully and firmly; and
- a simple but highly effective model for facilitating change that you can learn and implement.

The main therapeutic approach used in this book is rational emotive behaviour therapy (REBT), which was developed by the American psychologist Dr Albert Ellis.[1] As you go through the book, you'll discover that the main impediments to speaking your truth lie in your own mind. REBT has long been used to effectively identify and positively alter negative thought patterns and limiting beliefs that adversely affect a person's well-being and day-to-day life.

The basic tenets of REBT are as follows:

- Our thoughts, emotions, and behaviours are interrelated and significantly affect one another. What we think determines how we feel, which in turn affects how we behave.
- *What* happens to us is often not the issue; it is how we *interpret* the situation or event that determines how we feel and, subsequently, how we behave. The assumption here is

---

[1] Ellis, A., and Dryden W., *The Practice of Rational Emotive Behaviour Therapy*, 2nd ed., Free Association Books, London, 1999.

that it is our own unhealthy beliefs that keep us trapped in a certain way of being.
- We can learn how to identify, challenge, and change these unhealthy beliefs and thereby free ourselves to behave in a different way.

As a holistic practitioner, I work with all aspects of a person's being: their mental, emotional, physical, and spiritual selves. While REBT successfully engages and utilizes the amazing power of the human mind and emotions, with some issues the roots can lie deeper, in the more unconscious realms. For this reason, I have included a chapter at the end of this book on other simple energy-focused tools and approaches that can support you on your journey back to finding your voice.

The subject of this book is very close to my heart. I've come a long way since those early days of feeling afraid and disempowered, and I've had to overcome many internal obstacles to get here. Now I strive daily to speak my truth, and to speak it in a polite way. I don't always get it right, but I am a thousand times better at it than I was a decade ago. For example, now, I will challenge a person if he or she is speaking disrespectfully about someone I know. I don't automatically agree to take on additional responsibilities without first seriously considering the repercussions on my time, health, and family. And if I have something of value to say, no matter whom I'm speaking to, I say it with confidence. I no longer remain quiet.

Because I have been on this journey of discovery and learning myself, I know that it can initially feel scary. Learning to be assertive is like learning a new language. At the beginning, it can feel daunting and require an extra degree of effort. But as you begin to understand how you came to lose your voice in the first place, start to reflect on and challenge the underlying beliefs that are working against you, and learn alternative ways of expressing yourself, then in time being assertive will become second nature. It may be difficult at the beginning, but as with everything in life, the more you do it, the easier it gets.

Being assertive is about honouring and expressing your needs and desires in a way that is considerate of other people's needs and desires. As you'll discover in the next chapter, it does not mean getting your own way all the time. It's certainly not about shouting, arguing, or using your voice to abuse others—that's aggression, not assertiveness, and the two are entirely different. It's about learning to put your needs alongside those of others and mindfully and confidently speaking up for yourself in a manner that respects everyone concerned.

Throughout the book, you'll find references to five fictional characters who all struggle to be assertive in different situations in their lives. Aaron, Jasmine, Jay, Sharon, and Zara will be helping us to explore the issues that get in the way of a person speaking his or her truth and how these can be overcome. We will be following their individual journeys as each of them rediscovers his or her voice and learns to move from passivity to assertiveness. You will discover more about them as you go through the book, but for now, here is some background information about each of them.

Aaron

Aaron is a thirty-seven-year-old IT consultant. He's been married for fifteen years and has three young children. Aaron grew up in a large, chaotic family and has five siblings; he's the fourth child. He has an easygoing personality and a great sense of humour. He works hard and is a popular member of the IT team at work. Aaron loves music. He plays the guitar and has an extensive music collection, which he uses to relax and escape from the stresses and strains of everyday life.

Aaron feels his wife is domineering. She makes all the decisions in their life and is often critical of him. She particularly dislikes certain members of his family. Aaron finds it hard to make himself heard. He rarely expresses his true wishes and needs, and often feels frustrated and marginalized.

Jasmine

Jasmine is a thirty-two-year-old woman who works part-time in her local town council's human resources department. She is married, has two young children, and lives with her parents-in-law. Her husband's younger brother also lives with them. Jasmine's husband has a large, close-knit extended family. They host many social gatherings, with people regularly visiting the house.

Jasmine has a strong sense of style and prides herself on her appearance. She is very house-proud and always ensures that her home is immaculately clean and tidy. Jasmine is very mild-mannered. Her upbringing has taught her to be quiet, polite, and accommodating of others' needs. She takes her family responsibilities very seriously. Jasmine has recently been finding her work and family pressures difficult to handle and has started to experience anxiety attacks.

Jay

Jay is twenty-eight years old and works as an accounts assistant at a small firm. This is Jay's first job; he's been working at the company for six years. Jay is single and recently left home after a major disagreement with his father. Despite his anxieties about stepping onto the property ladder, he made the difficult decision to invest in a small studio apartment. He's mindful that he has a large mortgage and must be very careful with his money. He used to like going out with his friends, but owing to his limited finances he now finds himself staying at home most of the time.

At work, the annual pay review takes place entirely at the discretion of the business owner. Jay hasn't received a pay rise since starting at the company. He feels that he's worked hard and consistently met all his targets, and therefore deserves a pay rise. He believes that many of his colleagues have had their salaries increased, and he's starting to feel resentful.

Sharon

Sharon is forty-two years old and works as an administrative officer for a small charity. She is single and lives in a house share with two friends. Sharon had a disruptive childhood. Her father drank heavily, and her mother had mental health problems. They would often send Sharon to live with her elderly grandmother.

Sharon is kind, caring, and compliant by nature and finds it difficult to say no to any requests for help. She constantly finds herself taking on too much and often feels overwhelmed. Sharon has always been an avid reader. Recently, in an attempt to understand the low mood she often experiences, she has taken a keen interest in self-help books. She's realized that most of the people she helps don't seem to appreciate the time and energy she expends on them. She feels they take advantage of her good nature, and this is starting to upset her.

Zara

Zara is a thirty-five-year-old housewife. She is married to a successful businessman and has a young son. Zara's husband works long hours and is rarely at home. Zara dislikes this and would like him to spend more quality time with them. Her days are filled with housekeeping, cooking, the school run, and caring for her elderly mother, who lives nearby. Zara is a private person who struggles to express her feelings. As a child, she was bullied at school, and she prefers to keep herself to herself. Because she's always struggled to form and maintain relationships, she has no close friends.

Zara has been struggling with her weight for the past two years and has recently been diagnosed with an underactive thyroid gland (hypothyroidism). It's taken Zara some time to realize that she's been taking her anger at her husband out on their five-year-old son. She loses her temper easily and often shouts at him. Her son has now started to wet the bed.

I hope that as you read Aaron, Jasmine, Jay, Sharon, and Zara's stories, you'll be able to reflect on your own experiences of not speaking your truth and gain some insight into what holds you back from expressing yourself truthfully. To aid this process, I've included a series of self-reflection exercises throughout the book. These have been designed to encourage you to think about and uncover the underlying causes, and to identify the thoughts and beliefs that underpin your passivity with a view to moving past it.

The way we think and the beliefs we hold profoundly influence the way we feel and the way we behave. A crucial part of the journey from passivity to assertiveness is your identification and working through of the thoughts and beliefs that are keeping you locked into your passive behaviour. This is something you'll learn to do as you read on and work through the exercises, but for now I want to point out that one of the most powerful ways to pinpoint your innermost beliefs is through journaling. Writing down your thoughts and feelings opens you up to, and sheds light on, your internal dialogue—something that is difficult to do by merely thinking about an issue. For this reason, I strongly advise you to invest in a journal and make time to write down your thoughts in response to the self-reflection prompts included in this book.

If you can understand the core beliefs you hold, engage with the self-reflection questions in this book, work through the suggested exercises, and find the courage to try out the techniques shown in situations of your own choosing and at your own pace, you will find that gently, over time, you will have moved to that place of dignified, respectful, empowered expression that already exists somewhere deep inside of you.

1
Chapter

Understanding What Speaking Your Truth Really Means

As an experienced life coach and counsellor, I have the privilege of working with people who are proactively seeking to work through the difficulties they're experiencing in their everyday lives. I provide them with a safe, confidential, accepting space in which they can talk through the issues that are adversely affecting their sense of inner peace and well-being. My aim is to help them feel understood and less burdened. I support them to increase their self-awareness, self-confidence, and self-acceptance; to gain more clarity about their life situation; to enjoy healthier, more meaningful and fulfilling relationships; and to experience a greater degree of inner control. I also help them to gain an increased sense of personal power, joy, vitality, and fulfilment.

Many of my clients go through a process of personal transformation, and there often comes a point when I ask them if they speak their truth. Do they clearly communicate what they want? Do they tell their significant others how they feel? Do they make their expectations clear? From my years of working with clients, I've discovered that these questions commonly evoke two kinds of emotional response: confusion and fear.

It seems that many of my clients don't know what "speaking your truth" means, or else they misinterpret the phrase. Some assume it means being loud, forceful, and aggressive. Others think it means saying everything that comes into their mind with no regard for the consequences, no matter how inappropriate or negative it is. Some even believe it means revealing their private thoughts and feelings to everyone around them. Because these behaviours don't sit comfortably with most people, speaking their truth is a frightening prospect. They don't believe that this is who they are, and it's certainly not who they want to become, so they decide it's not for them.

However, speaking your truth means none of these things. It's certainly not about a hedonistic pursuit of your own needs to the constant detriment of others. It's not about insisting that you're right and others are wrong, or that your needs and desires are more important than anyone else's. Nor is it about arguing or acting superior in any way. It's not about telling everyone what you're thinking and feeling all the time. And it's certainly not about saying anything and everything that comes into your mind, with no regard for the repercussions.

Speaking your truth is essentially about being assertive. If we break it down and look at each of the constituent elements, it's about

- going inwards and connecting with your inner self;
- determining what your thoughts, feelings, and preferences are in any given situation (i.e., what you truly think, feel, and want);
- acknowledging the validity of these thoughts, feelings, and preferences;

- honestly communicating your thoughts, feelings, and preferences to others in a clear, calm, respectful way;
- choosing to communicate at a time that is appropriate; and
- not insisting that your preferences are the only ones that matter.

Assertiveness is very different to the misconceptions held by many. As Dr W Dryden and D Constantinou point out in their book *Assertiveness Step by Step*, lying right at the heart of assertiveness is the principle of equality and the regard for the delicate balance of power that exists between you and others in your life.[2] Learning to be assertive means accepting that we are all equal in worth, that we all have the right to be heard, and that we all deserve to have our needs met. It also means recognizing that the "all" in these statements includes you.

Learning how to speak your truth is fundamentally about understanding the power distribution in your relationships. It's about being self-aware. At one end of the spectrum, we have passive behaviour. This is where a person disowns his or her own power and cedes it to others. At the other end of the spectrum, we have aggressive behaviour, where a person snatches power from others and forcefully gets his or her way. A person who gives away his or her power may believe he or she has little or no influence, or control, over what happens in his or her life; this person may not have the confidence and self-trust to decide for himself or herself. A person who takes away power from others may believe he or she should be in complete control of what happens, and of other people, at all times; the person may believe he or she is entitled to decide for others and is in the right. The former is passive; the latter is dominant.

---

[2] Dryden, W., and Constantinou, D., *Assertiveness Step by Step* (Overcoming Common Problems series), Sheldon Press, London, 2004.

Passive Behaviour

Let's take a look at the characteristics of these opposing behaviours, starting with passive behaviour. Sharon, the forty-two-year-old charity worker we met earlier, is a good example.

Sharon displays passive behaviour in virtually every aspect of her life. People often ask her to do things for them, and even though she doesn't want to (and recognizes the fact that she doesn't want to), she still habitually says yes to all these requests. She continually fails to express her true feelings and desires in a clear, firm way, choosing instead to put others' needs before her own. She regularly gives away her power to others.

For example, Sharon lives with a housemate, Keira, who is particularly disorganized. Keira frequently gets up late in the morning and struggles to leave for work on time. On these occasions, she will ask Sharon to give her a lift to work. Driving Keira to work involves a twenty-minute detour for Sharon and potentially puts her at risk of being late for work herself. Despite the fact that this causes her stress, Sharon can't bring herself to refuse to drive Keira because she worries about her friend getting into trouble and then acting out her frustration on Sharon. She always reluctantly says yes. Sharon finds Keira's confident attitude somewhat intimidating and finds herself agreeing with much of what Keira asks of her.

Sharon's behaviour and attitude are typical of a passive person:

- She's afraid to speak up and say what she truly thinks and feels.
- She outwardly agrees with what others are saying even when she inwardly disagrees.
- She speaks very softly, and often in a rambling, hesitant, approval-seeking way.
- She avoids looking directly at people, slouches, and frequently looks down.

- She shows little or no emotion when talking to others, keeping her face and voice expressionless.
- She uses self-critical statements to belittle herself, her opinions, and her preferences.
- She values other people's thoughts, opinions, and desires more than her own.

Sharon's submissive, reticent behaviour makes it difficult for others to grasp what she is saying. It's also the reason people either misunderstand her views or simply dismiss them.

I can certainly identify with some of these characteristics when I look back on my younger self. My voice was so quiet that, even when I did pluck up the courage to say something, people often wouldn't hear me. I persistently shied away from expressing my true thoughts and opinions about everything. Instead I'd either say nothing or hypocritically agree with the views that others were expressing, even if they didn't accord with my own. It was a very disempowering period of my life.

Aggressive Behaviour

So what is the alternative? In my personal and professional experience, many people initially believe that the only alternative to passive behaviour must be aggressive behaviour. People fear that speaking their truth means being confrontational, loud, and antagonistic. They think that standing up for themselves and their needs means having to argue and fight with others. *It does not.* Just as there is a fundamental imbalance of power with passive behaviour, with aggressive behaviour the distribution of power is also out of balance.

Not only do aggressive people put their own needs and wishes above other people's, but they also demand that those needs are met. They often speak loudly, interrupt, and talk over others. Their body language is intimidating, and they invade other people's personal space. They make intense eye contact by glaring and staring at whomever they're interacting with, often speaking in a rigid, cold, patronizing tone. They're known for using condescending language. They don't listen, and they ignore or dismiss other people's points of view. They like to control situations and people, and they're good at manipulating outcomes so that they can constantly have their needs met, often to the detriment of others. This is certainly not what speaking your truth is about.

Assertive Behaviour

Speaking your truth is about being assertive, and this is entirely different to both passive and aggressive behaviour. Let's look at the characteristics of an assertive person.

An assertive person
- speaks openly and honestly about his or her preferences;
- has a steady, warm, conversational tone;
- maintains good eye contact and has a relaxed and open posture;
- uses "I" statements, such as "I prefer to ...", "I'd like to ...", and "I feel upset when ...";
- states his or her preferences in a clear and succinct way;
- cares about the preferences and opinions of those he or she is interacting with;
- listens to and considers other people's responses in a non-defensive way;
- considers himself or herself to be equal to others in his or her life; and
- believes he or she has the right to be heard and exercises that right in a way that is considerate of others.

We all know that relationships are complex. Our behaviour in any given situation is determined by a wide variety of factors, and it changes depending on how we feel in the moment, where we are, the person we're interacting with, and the circumstances we find ourselves in. We can all be passive, assertive, and aggressive at different times.

There will be some people who put you at your ease so that you can fully and openly express yourself. There will be others who bring out the aggressive side of your character. And there will be some people who are intimidating and overpowering, causing you to go into passive mode.

Self-Reflection Exercise 1: Knowing Where You Are Right Now

This is a good place for you to take some time to reflect on what your general default position is at the moment. Where along the spectrum of passive, assertive, and aggressive behaviour do you mostly operate?

Here are a few questions to help you to reflect:

- Q. In which areas of your life do you feel able to truly speak your mind?
- Q. Who are the people involved?
- Q. Do you share power equally with the people you've named, or is the power distributed unevenly between you?
- Q. In which areas of your life do you find it difficult to speak your truth?
- Q. Who are the people involved?
- Q. Do the people you've named in the second group exert power over you, or do you inadvertently give your power away?

It's a good idea to write down your answers in a journal. Writing is more powerful than merely thinking about something. Also, as you read on, there will be other self-reflection exercises for you to work through, so by writing down your responses, you'll be able to map your self-development journey.

As you go about your everyday life, notice how you feel and behave around different people and in different situations. Observe your emotions and behaviour as you interact with immediate family members, extended family, work colleagues, friends, and acquaintances when you're at home, at work, in social situations, or undertaking day-to-day activities, such as shopping. What do you discover about yourself? You may find that you identify patterns of behaviour that you weren't previously aware of. It is this self-knowledge that is going to be central to the transformation process you are embarking on, and therefore that will be our primary focus. Self-awareness really is the key to creating change. Our goal is to move you to a place within yourself where assertive behaviour is your default position, so it becomes the way you behave most of the time, irrespective of the situation and the people involved.

2

Chapter

The Origins of your Passive Behaviour

Have you ever wondered what makes you quiet and compliant? Were you just born that way, or is it a behaviour that you've learned? In this chapter, we are going to look at the possible explanations for passive behaviour. As with all human traits, it's often down to a complex combination of factors, some of which are rooted in nature and some in nurture.

Nature

People with certain personality types may be more likely to adopt passive behaviours. Elaine Aron, PhD, a clinical psychologist based in San Francisco, first identified the personality type "highly sensitive" in an academic paper she wrote in the early 1990s. She went on to write a bestselling book called *The Highly Sensitive Person: How to Thrive When the World Overwhelms You*, in which she estimates that highly sensitive people make up 15 to 20 per cent of the population.[3] She also states that those people are neurologically hard-wired differently to the rest of the population. Their nervous systems are much more sensitive to subtleties in their environments than those of their non-sensitive counterparts. Consequently, they can quickly become overstimulated. While we can't conclude that all passive people are highly sensitive, it's not unreasonable to assume that many are. And the reason is as follows.

Although the type of neurological wiring that comes with being sensitive can be considered a gift, because highly sensitive people are often very empathic, creative, and intuitive, there is a downside. Sensitive people can easily become overwhelmed. Things like noise, crowds, bright lights; chaotic, complex, or tense situations; and strained interactions with other people can leave them feeling tense and agitated. They often find themselves having to battle anxiety, depression, and low self-esteem as well. Consequently, as a way of protecting themselves, they learn to exercise greater self-care than non-sensitive people. And herein lies the link with passive behaviour: the constant fear and threat of being overwhelmed.

Passive behaviour can be a form of self-care, self-protection, and self-regulation. Highly sensitive people often take the path of least resistance in any given situation simply because they dislike the physiological changes that take place in their bodies when they're tense. When faced with a perceived threat or unnerving situation, such as an argument or the potential for strong disagreement with someone, their feelings of fear and discomfort can instantly evoke the fight-or-flight response.

The fight-or-flight response in the human body has been well documented. In the face of danger, real or imagined, a series of instant physiological changes occurs. These changes are designed

---

[3] Aron, E. N., *The Highly Sensitive Person: How to Thrive When the World Overwhelms You*, Thorsons, London, 1999.

to give the body a burst of energy and make it more responsive so it can deal with the perceived threat. The heart starts to beat faster, pushing blood to the muscles and other vital organs. Blood pressure goes up. Breathing becomes more rapid.[4] The smaller airways in the lungs widen to make more oxygen available, some of which is sent to the brain to increase alertness. Sight, hearing, and other senses sharpen. Temporary storage sites around the body release sugar and fats into the bloodstream to supply extra energy. The veins in the skin constrict to encourage more blood to flow to the major muscle groups, and muscles tense up, ready for action. Non-essential bodily functions, such as digestion and the immune response, temporarily shut down to provide more energy for the body to deal with the emergency. All these changes take place so that a person can either face the perceived threat (fight) or escape from it (flight).

The fight-or-flight wiring is so efficient that this cascade of changes begins even before the brain's visual centres have had a chance to fully process what's happening. This stress response is triggered so quickly that we're not consciously aware of it.

For a highly sensitive person, it is the merest perception of being under threat or in danger that can trigger this reaction, no matter how minuscule the risk may be. The instantaneous and involuntary nature of these physiological changes can be shocking, unpleasant and disorientating; it can bring on immediate and intense feelings of being overwhelmed.

Is it any wonder that a sensitive person would choose to avoid saying anything that another person might perceive as being confrontational? Either consciously or unconsciously, sensitive people perceive many situations and people as threatening. They figure it's wiser to smile and agree with whatever people around them are suggesting rather than disagree and risk a confrontation.

---

[4] Cannon, W., *The Wisdom of the Body*, W.W. Norton & Company Inc., New York, 1963.

It's easier to avoid difficult situations, ignore things, back away, and withdraw than to deal with people and problems head-on, because that way they don't have to deal with their own discomfort. It's easy to see how sensitive people learn at an early age that it's far simpler and less stressful to keep their heads down and their mouths shut.

Nurture

Our upbringing is another factor that affects the way we interact with other people. The verbal and non-verbal messages we receive as children play a key role in defining our behaviour and sense of self as an adult.

When we are young, we're taught how to interact with others, and through this process of socialisation we learn to fit into the world we find ourselves in. If we're to successfully integrate into our families, our communities, and society in general, we must learn the rules of acceptable behaviour, and we must obey them. This naturally demands a certain degree of compliance and passivity.

There is one thing that we human beings have in common: we all crave positive regard from others. This is particularly so in childhood. In order to develop a healthy sense of self and a sense of self-worth, we need acknowledgement, love, and acceptance. What's more, we all want to fit in with our family, peers, and community. The young ego pays great heed to the opinions that others have of it and actively seeks approval, while strenuously avoiding disapproval.

As young children, we quickly learn that, firstly, we must earn positive regard from others and, secondly, that this positive regard is usually conditional. If we want other people to accept and like us, then we must *behave in a certain way*. For example, biting, hitting, and snatching are all behaviours that attract disapproval. Most adults will ensure a toddler knows this very early on. Similarly, as we grow older, the expected norms of behaviour are made clear to us. Families, for example, often have clearly defined expectations of behaviour, and each generation attempts to pass on these norms and values to the next generation, either explicitly, through direct instruction, or implicitly, through modelling or overt signs of disapproval, such as the withdrawal of attention or love. Manners are a good example. I grew up in a household where I was actively taught to greet people when I first saw them in the morning, to say "thank you" and "please", to lend a hand with the household chores, and to clear up after myself. If I didn't do these things, I would be told off. Schools do the same. These institutions expend considerable energy encouraging, and even coercing, teenagers to follow rules and respect authority. In a bid to win approval, most children learn to mould their behaviour to fit these expectations at an early age. While such learned behaviour does not in and of itself lead directly to passivity later in life, when combined with a sensitive personality it certainly encourages a more compliant and passive attitude.

Jasmine, the thirty-two-year-old mother and wife who lives with her husband's family, is a good example of someone who grew up with this sort of conditioning. She was raised in a family in which there were many conditions attached to the positive regard she received from her parents. Her parents gave her the message loud and clear that she had to behave and live her life in a certain way if she wanted others to accept and love her. She had to speak politely at all times. She had to respect and obey her elders. She had to meet other people's needs before she considered her own. She had to conduct herself in a calm, respectful, controlled manner, especially when around other people or outside the house. As a teenager, she wasn't allowed to drink alcohol or smoke, and she certainly wasn't allowed to associate with boys. If she ever became loud, boisterous, overexcited, or angry, she was severely chastised. If she ever arrived home late from school, she would be grilled on where and with whom she had been. Although on the surface Jasmine's childhood and everyday life were comfortable, and her parents behaved lovingly towards her, they made it perfectly clear that if she didn't comply with their rules and behave in the way they expected of her, the consequences would be severe. They would withdraw their love and support; she would be disowned, and she would be disgraced within her extended family and community.

Jasmine internalized these expectations at a young age, and they subsequently shaped her choices and conduct as an adult. She knew that she had to get a good education, get married to someone her family approved of, have children, support her husband, manage the household, look after her parents-in-law, contribute to the family finances, and accommodate the needs of not only her husband's family but the extended family as well. And not only did she have to do all this, but she had to do it happily and willingly, with a smile, so that she didn't make other people uncomfortable. She was aware that her place was in the home and that aside from going out to work, she should not pursue friendships and socialize with people outside of the family. Having a social life would be an unnecessary distraction from her responsibilities and would be frowned upon. Jasmine was conditioned to keep her views and opinions to herself, especially if they were different to those around her, and to be obedient and polite at all times. She learned to behave in this way so she would fit in and not upset the status quo. The message Jasmine had heard throughout her younger life was that if she didn't do so, she would be rejected by those around her. She had seen other defiant young women who refused to comply with the restrictions placed upon them become the targets of vicious gossip and be ostracized from the community; this filled her with horror. The threat of disapproval from her family and community acted as a strong deterrent for Jasmine; it ensured that she conformed and behaved in a passive way.

Another way in which we learn how to behave and manage our inner and outer worlds is by watching and modelling our parents and caregivers. If you're fortunate enough to be brought up in a home where the adults (a) offer their love, care, and attention openly and unconditionally; (b) provide an emotionally safe and secure environment for you to learn and develop in; and (c) show you how to handle your emotions by dealing with their own emotions in a balanced and healthy way, then you are more likely to develop a healthy sense of self and an effective set of strategies for managing your inner world. On the other hand, if your parents aren't comfortable with their own emotions and believe it's better to hide their true feelings, then you will learn that it's not acceptable for you to express your true thoughts and feelings at any time.

The way a family deals with anger is usually typical of how it deals with emotional issues in general. Zara is a thirty-five-year-old housewife with a young son. She grew up in a home where emotions were rarely expressed, outwardly acknowledged, or talked about. Her mother is a quiet, dignified woman who kept herself emotionally distant from Zara. As a child, Zara never saw her mother raise her voice or express anger in any way. She did know when her mother was upset however; she would simply shut herself away or go silent. Zara knew to stay away from her during those times. Her mother modelled a way of reacting to emotional distress that Zara unconsciously learned and carried into adulthood. Now, whenever she experiences any emotional difficulty, Zara too withdraws into herself and literally shuts down all communication with others.

Growing up in a family that does not, or cannot, attach much value to your basic needs and desires suppresses your natural impulse to say what you want, need, and feel. If your caregivers are too busy to listen when you try to talk to them about your desires, you may learn that there's no point in voicing those desires. If when you assert yourself you're told to "stop thinking about yourself" or "not be so selfish", then you may learn that your needs and desires are unacceptable and that you must ignore them. If you're raised by a parent or caregiver who expresses his or her emotions inappropriately or aggressively—violently even—then that, too, may create a conditioned response, leading you to decide early on that it's not safe for you to express your true feelings, especially if they're negative ones.

Sharon grew up in a dysfunctional home. Her father's drinking and her mother's mental health issues meant that no one was emotionally available for her. Her parents often made her feel as though she were a burden. Her mother would constantly complain about having to get up early to take Sharon to school. On many mornings, she'd spend the entire journey scolding Sharon for not being able to get there herself, even as a very young child. She'd grumble about having to provide food for her and having to stay at home to look after her, even though she performed these tasks inadequately most of the time. Her father was physically and emotionally abusive and would shout at her and slap her for no apparent reason. The constant threat of random violence left Sharon feeling highly anxious and alone. She learnt at a very young age that it was best if she stayed quiet and hidden from view. She realized that the bond she had with her parents was extremely tenuous, so she learned to cultivate an attitude of passivity and compliance. Her survival depended on it. This pattern was reinforced further when she went to live with her elderly grandmother. While her grandmother provided a safe, loving home, Sharon was acutely aware of her age and frailty and noticed that at times she struggled to look after her. Sharon knew that if she asked for more attention than her grandmother could give her, she would be sent back home to her parents. She knew she had to cooperate and not be a nuisance. Her experience with her parents had caused her to internalize the message that her needs, opinions, and preferences were not important, so she learnt to be as quiet and obedient as she could be.

Self-Reflection Exercise 2: Getting to Know Yourself Better

As we've seen, passive behaviour can have its origins in your innate nature and your upbringing. If you are to begin the process of personal change, you need to start by gaining a certain degree of self-awareness. By reflecting on your character, feelings, motives, desires, and past experiences, you will arrive at a better understanding of yourself and the reasons why you act in the ways you do. Here are some questions to help you with this:

- Q. Do you recognize within yourself any of the characteristics attributed to highly sensitive people? For example, are you easily overwhelmed by such things as bright lights, strong smells, coarse fabrics, or nearby sirens? Do you get tense when you have a lot to do in a short amount of time? Do you make a point of avoiding violent movies and TV shows? Do you regularly need quiet time by yourself, especially when you've had a busy day? Do you find yourself organizing your life so as to avoid upsetting or overwhelming situations?
- Q. How did your parents expect you to behave when you were a child? For example, what kinds of behaviours were rewarded and what kinds of behaviours were frowned upon?
- Q. How comfortable do you feel expressing your emotions?
- Q. How comfortable are your parents or caregivers with expressing their emotions?
- Q. When you spoke about your needs and desires as a child, what kinds of reactions did you receive?

As before, it's best to record your responses in a journal.

3
Chapter

Why Speaking Your Truth Matters

One of our shared traits as human beings is that we only ever engage in behaviours that we consciously or subconsciously believe lead to positive outcomes. In the short term, the direct consequences of not speaking your truth seem to be quite advantageous. By remaining quiet and docile, you're able to avoid any discomfort. The threat of confrontation and conflict is immediately eliminated. You remove the risk of being judged, disliked, and disapproved of. Your behaviour keeps other people happy. And you also eradicate the likelihood of hurting another person's feelings. It's not difficult to see how refraining from speaking your truth makes life easier and more pleasant for everyone involved.

So why would you want to change? Why would you even bother to read this book? After all, learning a new way of thinking and behaving takes considerable energy; you will need to invest time and inner resources on self-reflection, and muster up the focus and discipline required to learn a new skill. You will also need to find the courage to implement this new learning in your everyday life. Is it worth the trouble? *It most certainly is.*

Here's why. Although behaving passively seems like the best approach initially, in the long term it can have a devastating effect on your sense of identity, your confidence, and your relationships. Failing to speak your truth doesn't just damage your mental and emotional health; it also has a detrimental effect on your physical and spiritual well-being. As you read on, you may be surprised to learn how wide-ranging the impact can be.

Self-Esteem

The single most destructive effect of not speaking your truth is the impact it has on your sense of self (i.e. your self-esteem). This is your perception of who you are and your belief in your own worth. If you go through life never saying what you really feel or think, always agreeing with others, and always seeking to fulfil their needs and desires, you soon lose all sense of who you truly are—and before long, you find yourself living a life that doesn't belong to you. Not only do you lose touch with your true self, but you also lose control of your own life.

Every time you choose to remain quiet and not express your true thoughts and feelings, you're sending a clear message to yourself that you're not important—that you're not equal to, or as worthy as, those around you. Whenever you denigrate your own opinions and preferences, you are elevating the needs and wishes of other people in your life above your own. You're giving other people more importance and judging them to be worthier than yourself. You're acting as if they're superior—as though they have more of a right to be heard and to have their preferences met than you do. The self receives the message loud and clear: *I don't matter; my opinions, thoughts and feelings don't count; I'm not worthy of time, attention, or consideration.* This leads to a very unhealthy, ever-diminishing sense of self that ultimately crystallizes into a set of damaging core beliefs. And we know that our core beliefs strongly influence our thoughts, feelings, and behaviour at an unconscious level.

Sharon, for example, rarely says what she truly thinks and feels. She is constantly "people-pleasing" and says yes to everything that's asked of her. On the odd occasion that she does try to express an opinion, she does so in such a weak, timid way that people simply don't hear her, or they dismiss out of hand what she's said. For instance, when Sharon's friend asks her to babysit at the last minute so she can attend a training event, Sharon's immediate response is, "Yes, no problem." But her words couldn't be further from the truth, because Sharon has already made plans for the day. It is, in fact, a problem for her, because now she must put her own plans on hold and take care of her friend's child. Sharon knows full well that she dislikes babysitting; the responsibility overwhelms her. But despite this, she still finds it preferable to comply with her friend's request. She decides, on some level, that it's easier to keep her real feelings to herself. Let's consider why that is.

Firstly, Sharon doesn't want to let down, upset, or offend her friend, because doing so would make Sharon feel bad about herself. Secondly, by saying yes, she avoids the discomfort of coming into conflict with her friend. On several occasions, Sharon has witnessed her friend become irritable and rude when she hasn't gotten get her own way. This frightens Sharon and makes her feel anxious. Agreeing with her friend's wishes means that Sharon doesn't have to face her own anxiety—she has evaded the threat of discord, however small. Thirdly, by acquiescing, Sharon avoids the feelings of guilt she often experiences when she puts her own needs above those of others.

Prioritizing these short-term gains has, however, had a detrimental effect on Sharon over the long term; it has affected her happiness, her sense of self, and her confidence. Over time, Sharon's opinion of herself has deteriorated to such an extent that she now believes she's not worthy of respect and attention. She believes it's not possible for her to do as she pleases; her life is about everyone else and what they need and desire. She's reached a point at which she doubts she even has the capacity to stand up for herself and say what she truly wants. Years of passive behaviour have created the belief that she can't change; her passivity has become a part of her self-identity. It has also become her default mode of behaviour—so much so that she doesn't even question it. Furthermore, in attempting to avoid external conflict, Sharon finds herself in a perpetual state of internal conflict. In this case, she has to deal with the discordant feelings of being inwardly compelled to agree to the babysitting request and not wanting to. Sharon's passive and compliant stance has led to her living a more restricted life than she has to, simply because she doesn't say and do what she wants. She has lost her own sense of direction and autonomy because she's constantly people-pleasing.

Passive behaviour not only does serious harm to who you believe you are but also sends out unhealthy messages to other people in your life. When you don't respect yourself by saying what you do and don't want, you're consciously and unconsciously telling others, "You have permission not to respect me either."

Sharon's friend knows that Sharon will never say no to any requests for help simply because she has never done so in the past. She always says, "No problem." By consistently behaving in a passive way, Sharon has taught her friend to expect that from her. Speaking your truth is ultimately about respecting yourself. It's about honouring who you are and how you feel, and ensuring that others honour you too.

Self-Direction

It doesn't take a great leap of imagination to see that when you consistently ignore your own needs and wishes and go along with the needs and wishes of the significant others in your life, you eventually end up living a life that is controlled and directed by someone else. If you constantly allow another person to get away with not listening to you and not considering your needs, you quickly end up living that person's life and not your own. By handing over your power in this way, you not only lose control over your existence; you also lose your identity. This can have a devastating effect on your health and happiness.

Aaron is a good example of someone who's lost his sense of self-direction and self-autonomy. Aaron's wife dislikes his siblings. Over the years, she's managed to distance herself and Aaron from them to such a point that he rarely sees them. In the early stages of their marriage, Aaron tried to assert himself, but whenever he did so, he faced a hostile reaction. This deterred him from bringing up the subject again. Initially, appeasing his wife seemed like a good idea. It avoided friction between them, and Aaron didn't have to listen to her constant disapproval. He did have conflicting feelings about not seeing his siblings, but he eventually succumbed to his wife's dominant personality, in a bid to keep her happy. But now he misses seeing his family, and the situation has become a source of much frustration and sadness in his life. Aaron feels that he must choose between a quiet life with his wife and his own wish to share his life with his siblings.

At a deeper level, Aaron has turned some of the anger he feels about the situation onto himself. He knows that he should have taken a stand and not allowed his wife to dictate whom he can and cannot see. As Aaron has continually allowed her to treat him in this manner, she has grown accustomed to getting her own way. She now controls virtually everything in his life to such a degree that Aaron has given up trying to express his wishes altogether. This has eroded his sense of self, his self-respect, and his confidence. He often feels low in mood and has lost his zest for life.

Self-Respect

Our ability to speak up and be assertive is directly linked to the amount of respect we have for ourselves. You may think that being quiet and not rocking the boat will cause other people to approve of you and will make you feel good about yourself. But what you're actually doing is sending a signal to others that you don't respect yourself; and every time you behave passively, you erode your self-respect further. The paradox is that although passive behaviour is initially about getting approval and respect from others, this is rarely what transpires. You may believe that by being continually accommodating and compliant, you will gain a degree of positive regard. But the exact opposite happens: respect and approval are the last things you earn by being passive. When you don't respect yourself enough to be honest about your needs and desires, when you refuse to speak up and express yourself appropriately, you give others free reign to, at best, ignore you and, at worst, disrespect and control you.

Jay's inability to speak up for himself at work, especially about his salary, has resulted in him having a poor self-image. In his case, this has created feelings of resentment towards others. He projects his own feelings of inadequacy onto his colleagues and feels bitter about their successes and progress. Instead of dealing with the issues directly with the people involved, he makes disparaging remarks about his manager and peers behind their backs and has now acquired a reputation for being somewhat unpleasant. His colleagues have lost respect for him, and this in turn has further damaged his already low sense of self-worth. Ironically, this behaviour has probably also lowered his chances of getting the pay rise and promotion he so desperately craves.

Stress and Anxiety

Another common issue with passive behaviour is stress. If you repeatedly say yes to everything that's asked of you, you will invariably take on too much. This can quickly lead to feelings of being overwhelmed, tension, and anxiety. When you constantly refrain from communicating your limits, opinions, and feelings to those around you, it's not long before you begin to feel trapped and experience the negative impact of this behaviour on your health.

Jasmine's upbringing has taught her to be passive. She believes her role in life is to be obedient, dutiful, and quiet. She manages the entire household: the grocery shopping, the cleaning, the cooking, and the laundry. She goes out to work and looks after her children. She's also expected to welcome guests to the house whenever they want to visit and attend numerous family gatherings. Not only that, but she feels she must do all of this with a smile on her face because that's what others expect of her. Jasmine rarely has a day off from her "duties"; her upbringing has led her to not allow it. She constantly does what she believes she should be doing, rather than what she wants to do. As a result, she has become alienated from who she truly is and what she truly wants.

As the gulf between her ideal self (i.e., the image she holds in her mind about who she should be) and her authentic self grows bigger, Jasmine begins to experience deep inner turmoil. The conflict and tension between these two parts of her being eventually manifest as serious attacks of anxiety. By always doing what she believes to be the right thing and constantly people-pleasing, Jasmine has inadvertently locked herself in an inner world from which she sees no way out. This is an inner world where her thoughts and feelings are dictated by how she *should* behave, rather than how she naturally *wants* to behave. Furthermore, the expectations she places on herself are so high that they're impossible to maintain all the time. Every now and again, she inevitably falls short of her own standards and then feels bad about herself. Is it any wonder that she feels overwhelmed and anxious? Joy, passion, and energy come from a person's true nature. Jasmine's life is so full of duty and obligation that she has become alienated from herself. She doesn't know who she is, what she enjoys doing, or what her passion is in life.

Relationships with Others

In addition to damaging your relationship with yourself, not speaking your truth has a serious and destructive impact on your relationship with others. With Jay and Sharon, we've already touched on how passive behaviour can lead to relationships that are unhealthy and uncomfortable. If we take a closer look at Zara's experience, we can see just how much distress such behaviour can cause. As well as undermining her own health and happiness, Zara's passive behaviour also has negative consequences for her family's mental, emotional, and physical well-being.

Zara rarely speaks her truth. Instead she expects her husband to "just know" how she feels. She expects him to know what she wants without telling him. Since her husband is not a mind reader, he often gets it wrong and says and does things that irritate her. Instead of expressing her irritation through honest and clear communication, she leaves it to fester inside. Internalizing and suppressing this energy has turned it into deep, unarticulated anger.

Anger is an emotion that needs to be addressed. It is an attack energy that, left unexpressed and unresolved, can turn on the self, leading to depression and physical disease. It can also warp a person's personality over time, making him or her behave in a passive-aggressive manner.

Passive-aggressive behaviour takes many forms but is basically a non-verbal aggression that manifests as negative behaviour. Such behaviour results when you are angry with someone but do not, or cannot, tell him or her. Instead of communicating honestly when you feel upset, annoyed, unhappy, or disappointed, you bottle up your feelings, shut off verbally, give angry looks, make obvious changes to your behaviour, make inexplicit negative comments, act obstructively, sulk, or put up a stonewall. Passive-aggressiveness is a destructive, emotionally abusive pattern of behaviour. It eats away at trust in a relationship and creates intense negative energy, which causes pain to all parties.

Zara displays passive-aggressive behaviour towards her husband. She feels angry at him for staying late at work, for not spending time with their son, and for not being there for her. However, instead of talking about how she feels and making her needs and wishes known to him, she behaves in an unpleasant way. She gives her husband the silent treatment. She stomps around the house banging doors. She makes snide comments about minor issues. It's obvious to Zara's husband that something is wrong, but every time he tries to talk to her, she refuses to be truthful about her feelings. Instead she covers up the real reason for her unhappiness by blaming it on other things. The underlying issues remain unresolved.

Zara's behaviour has resulted in an accumulation of toxic energy between her and her husband, between her and her son, and within herself. She suffers from a range of physical health problems, including a thyroid problem, hypertension, and muscular aches and pains. Children can be particularly sensitive to the energy in their environment, and negative energy can affect their mental, emotional, and physical health. Zara's five-year-old son senses the tense atmosphere in the family home but is too young to be able to understand or articulate his thoughts and feelings about the situation. As a result of the stress, he has started to wet the bed.

If you don't express your needs, then they simply remain unmet. People can't read your mind. If you don't communicate your thoughts and feelings honestly, clearly, and openly, then how will others know what you want and need? You may think the problem is self-evident, but we all live life subjectively. The people around you may interpret the situation and read the signals differently. You need to take responsibility for expressing your views as clearly and as honestly as you can.

Another far-reaching consequence of not speaking our truth calmly, openly, and honestly is that we teach our children to keep their thoughts and feelings bottled up too. Parents are role models for their children. Children learn more from parental behaviour than parental instruction. If, as parents, we don't demonstrate that we're communicating our thoughts and feelings effectively in a healthy, balanced way, then it will be more difficult for our children to do so as well.

Remaining passive doesn't benefit anyone in the long term—neither you nor others in your life. As you've learnt, passiveness can affect the quality of every aspect of your inner and outer life, and the quality of the lives of the people around you, in a profoundly negative way. It makes it virtually impossible to lead a happy, fulfilled, purposeful life. If you don't honour and communicate your truth to others, not only do you let yourself down, but you also do a disservice to others by not giving them a fair chance to help you meet your needs. You end up devaluing yourself and resenting others. As your needs continue to be unfulfilled, it's not long before you conclude that *no one cares*. This erodes your sense of self even further and perpetuates the downward spiral that ultimately leads to physical, emotional, mental, and spiritual illness. Ask yourself, can you really afford not to speak your truth?

Self-Reflection Exercise 3: Understanding How Being Passive Affects Your Life

Take some time to reflect on how your passive behaviour may have adversely affected your life. Think about each of the themes covered in this chapter (self-esteem, self-direction, self-respect, stress and anxiety, and your relationships) and write down your thoughts in your journal.

Here are some questions to help you reflect.

- Q. How does your passive behaviour make you feel about yourself?
- Q. How does your passive behaviour affect the level of control you feel you have over your life?
- Q. How does your passive behaviour affect your ability to live your life in accordance with your own goals, dreams, and wishes?
- Q. What signals do you think your passive behaviour sends to the significant others in your life?
- Q. How does your passive behaviour affect these key relationships?
- Q. How does your passive behaviour affect your general stress levels?

4
Chapter

What You Stand to Gain by Speaking Your Truth

There are only ever two reasons why we're motivated to change our behaviour. We're either driven to move away from something we don't like so that we can avoid pain (real or perceived), or we're inspired to move towards something we want that will bring us benefit or pleasure (real or perceived). In the previous chapter, we looked at how damaging passive behaviour can be and why we would want to move away from it. In this chapter, we're going to explore the benefits of assertive behaviour and the reasons we would want to move towards it. So what do you stand to gain by finding your voice and speaking your truth?

Greater Self-Awareness

First off, recognizing and understanding your feelings means that you can start to be true to yourself. When you choose to be assertive, not only do you develop greater self-awareness but you also cultivate greater self-respect. Self-awareness is the first step to being assertive. Before you can express your feelings and opinions, you need to recognize and acknowledge what they are. And then, as you become more willing to express your feelings to others, there emerges a new respect for yourself—the kind that comes only from being truthful about how you feel. You realize that you have a right to your own opinion, and you also have the right to express that opinion.

The more assertive you become, the more clarity you gain about who you really are. When you are assertive, you're more aware of your identity, your values, your beliefs, your likes, and your dislikes, simply because being assertive requires you to look inside and recognize these aspects of yourself. This increased self-awareness leads to a healthier, more respectful relationship with yourself, which in turn helps to boost self-confidence and self-esteem. Being assertive, therefore, powerfully enhances your self-image.

Garnered Respect

Secondly, assertiveness earns you respect from others. When you have a high degree of self-awareness and high self-esteem, you're able to extend that courtesy to others. You understand others better, you become more empathic, and, consequently, you engage with others in a more positive and respectful way. As mentioned earlier, assertiveness is based on the principle of equality and maintaining the delicate balance of power in your relationships and interactions with others. As you learn to view others in a more respectful way and emanate a powerful sense of self-respect, you automatically invite greater respect from those around you.

Improved Relationships

All these factors lead to the third benefit: improved relationships. Learning to be assertive means learning a healthier style of communication—one that is clear and unambiguous. As you learn to express your needs, wants, and feelings in a well-defined and calm way, and as you learn to listen to and consider the other person's needs, wants, and feelings, you naturally increase the chances of each party feeling heard and understood. Assertiveness helps everyone arrive at a win-win situation. It naturally decreases the probability of conflicts and arguments, while increasing feelings of mutual respect and promoting openness and honesty in relationships.

Reduced Anxiety

Fourthly, learning to be assertive reduces anxiety and increases a person's sense of freedom and autonomy. The ability to truly reflect on how you feel about any given situation, and the willingness to say no when you're unable to comply with requests for your time, energy, and expertise, mean that as an assertive person you'll be less anxious than people who are passive. Assertive people do not become overwhelmed with the pressure that results from taking on too much. They don't have to manage the difficult thoughts and feelings that inevitably arise whenever they do what they feel they *should* do, as opposed to that which they *choose* to do. Assertiveness stops other people living your life for you and frees up your time and energy for things that truly matter to you. It allows you to take back control of your own life and make your own decisions so you can live your life on your own terms. This brings about a sense of freedom and control that a passive person simply cannot have.

Healthier Spirit

Finally, speaking your truth in a kind, respectful way can be a spiritual practice. We all have the essence of Spirit within us. Many people are exceptionally good at honouring that essence in others, but very few extend this courtesy to themselves. For example, we listen to others' needs and wishes yet often ignore our own. We pay other people compliments yet denigrate our own bodies, personalities, and talents. We show other people compassion and kindness but treat ourselves harshly when it comes to our own shortcomings.

To connect with, value, and express your authentic self is to live your life in alignment with your spiritual essence. Passion for life, joy, and energy emanate from the deepest part of your being. Losing touch with your spiritual core and denying your truth means living in a false world, alienated from who you truly are. When you withhold your truth, you close off a part of yourself, and in doing so, you block the flow of vital energy (that which gives you life) within you. Not only does this leave you feeling depressed; it also drains you as you expend precious life force energy suppressing valuable parts of yourself.

Speaking your truth in a fearless but compassionate way connects you to the highest part of your being, generates a vibrant aliveness, and frees you to live life to your full potential. It is in the sharing of your deepest truth with another that you create the space for more love and freedom to enter your life.

I know that when I started to speak my truth, my life became considerably less burdensome. I felt less anxious, less overwhelmed, and in far more control of what I did and when I did it. When I allowed myself the time and space to acknowledge my true thoughts and feelings about any situation I faced, and then shared those thoughts and feelings with others, my life began to feel as if it belonged to me. When I no longer responded in the way that others expected of me (for example, by constantly pandering to their every whim or persistently reorganizing my life to accommodate their wishes) but instead came from a place of personal truth and power, I saw that people treated me with greater respect. They valued my opinions and preferences and respected my boundaries. And, over time, all this has significantly enhanced my self-esteem. It's made me feel good about myself—and my life.

Self-Reflection Exercise 4: Envisaging How Speaking Your Truth Could Improve Your Life

Having read this chapter and discovered the ways in which speaking truthfully and assertively can enhance a person's life, spend some time reflecting on your personal situation. In your journal, write down the ways in which your life could improve, and how your sense of self could benefit, if you learnt to be more assertive. What would you stand to gain by finding your voice and speaking your truth? You may find it helpful to write about the various areas mentioned in this chapter: self-awareness and self-confidence, respect, relationships, well-being, and spirituality.

Chapter 5

Why You Are Afraid to Speak Up

We all like to believe that when it comes to speaking our truth, the obstacles that stand in our way are placed there by other people; it's the belligerent boss, the difficult mother-in-law, the absent husband, the cantankerous wife, or whoever else may challenge us that is the problem. The reality, however, is that we get in our own way. It's important to realize that the only person stopping you from speaking your truth is *you*. It's true that in certain situations, such as when you're dealing with people in positions of authority (teachers and managers, for example) or overly aggressive or unpredictable people, it can be more difficult to be assertive, but if passivity has become your habitual behaviour with everyone, then the issues clearly lie within you.

The journey from passiveness to assertiveness starts with one basic step: a willingness to identify, understand, and address the *fears and unhealthy beliefs* that you're holding on to deep inside.

Beliefs are personal evaluations that derive from your experience and your perception of yourself, other people, and the world around you. You use them to make sense of the world and your place in it. Your beliefs are important because they profoundly *influence your emotions and behaviour.* Healthy beliefs fuel healthy feelings and behaviour, while unhealthy beliefs fuel unhealthy feelings and behaviour.

With the help of our fictional characters, let's explore the most common fears around assertiveness. As these examples will show, many of our most powerful beliefs and fears stem from our childhood experiences.

Jay's Fears

Jay has an annual review with his manager, and every year he struggles to ask for a pay rise. He's worked at the company for six years and in this time has watched other people negotiate promotions and rise through the ranks. But Jay has been stuck at the same position and salary since he started. Jay's inability to speak up for himself can be traced back to a number of fears:

- **The fear of losing his job:** He has a large mortgage and can't afford to be out of work. He's also had a major disagreement with his father and feels he can never return to live in the family home; his pride won't allow it.
- **The fear of not being good enough:** He feels lucky to have found this job in the first place and is worried he won't be able to secure another one.
- **The fear of being "found out":** He thinks that if he draws attention to himself, his manager will realize he is not competent at his job.

- **The fear of rejection:** He's certain that his boss will refuse to increase his pay even if he does summon the courage to ask; and what's more, he feels that when he's found out, he will almost certainly be asked to leave.
- **The fear of being ignored:** He can't bear the thought of further injury to his already damaged sense of self. He's scared it will confirm that other people don't think he's worth taking seriously.
- **The fear of taking on extra responsibility:** He just wants an easy life. A pay award could lead to additional duties, which he doesn't want.

This collection of unhealthy beliefs creates a range of negative emotions in Jay. Whenever he thinks about speaking up in his pay review meeting, he feels the physical symptoms of fear. The mere thought of it causes him to feel butterflies in his stomach. He begins to feel hot and clammy, his breathing becomes faster and shallower, and his voice begins to shake. Moreover, these uncomfortable and disturbing sensations fuel feelings of embarrassment, despair, and anger. It's not surprising, then, that Jay chooses to remain silent.

Initially he turns these feelings inwards, towards himself; but then, almost despite himself, he begins to direct them at his boss and colleagues through his passive-aggressive behaviour. For example, he stops pulling his weight when it comes to team assignments and fails to meet deadlines for which he is responsible. He refuses to cooperate with members of his team, and he begins to make disparaging remarks about his boss and colleagues to anyone who will listen.

Jasmine's Fears

Jasmine's compliant behaviour stems from an underlying belief that her reputation (i.e., the opinion that others hold of her) is of paramount importance. She worries about how the people in her life—her parents-in-law, husband, brother-in-law, and her own parents—will perceive her behaviour if she doesn't meet their expectations. This belief feeds into a whole raft of fears, which in turn guide and influence her behaviour:

- **The fear of disapproval:** If she says and does what she wants, those closest to her will criticize her.
- **The fear of judgement:** Not only will they label her behaviour as bad, but worse still, they'll see her as a bad person.
- **The fear of rejection:** They'll be so disappointed in her that they'll shun her altogether and leave her on her own.
- **The fear of criticism:** They'll voice their disapproval so she knows she's done wrong, and they'll most likely complain about her to others.
- **The fear of feeling like a failure:** She has internalized other people's expectations of her and how she should live her life to such an extent that the thought of not meeting those expectations makes her feel like a catastrophic failure.
- **The fear of letting others down:** She can't bear the thought of upsetting the people she loves the most—her husband and her parents—by failing to meet their expectations.
- **The fear of being selfish:** She believes that good people focus on others' needs and not their own.

Because of her fears, Jasmine's entire focus is located outside of herself—in the people that are important to her and the ways in which they react to her. It's not difficult to see how these fears act as powerful and rigid constraints. Even if Jasmine wants to do things differently, her beliefs keep her locked into her passive behaviour.

Jasmine's *fear of her own emotional and physical reactions* further reinforces her quiet, compliant behaviour. She's been experiencing bouts of anxiety recently that leave her feeling frightened and out of control. For instance, she found herself panicking one day when her mother-in-law unexpectedly asked her to pick up something from the local shop. She was already feeling overwhelmed with her busy schedule that day and didn't have time to fit in the extra trip. But, at the same time, she couldn't refuse the request. When for a moment she thought about saying no, she felt her stomach tense up, her heart began to beat faster, and she had difficulty breathing. She became physically and emotionally uncomfortable to the point that the fear of her own discomfort made it easier to just agree and do as her mother-in-law had asked.

Like most of us, Jasmine dislikes discomfort and naturally avoids situations and interactions that could trigger the adrenaline-fuelled fight-or-flight response described in chapter 2. The fear of triggering an anxiety attack, and the physical discomfort of the body's natural stress response, is enough to deter Jasmine from doing anything that might potentially result in conflict. It's so much easier for her to agree with everyone and comply, no matter how inconvenient it is for her.

Aaron's Fears

Aaron has an easy-going, non-confrontational personality and prefers to go with the flow. This is a strategy that generally works well for him. A closer look at Aaron's underlying beliefs highlights several deep-seated fears and explains why he chooses to maintain a permanently passive stance in all his dealings with others.

Growing up in a large family, Aaron relied on others to take responsibility for his everyday life. His parents and older siblings took care of all his daily needs, which meant that he never had to fend for himself or even make many decisions for himself. Aaron fell in love with, and chose to marry, a woman who allowed him to continue this same pattern of laid-back behaviour into his adult life. His wife is happy to take the lead, and this suits Aaron perfectly because he gets to have an easy life. He doesn't have to deal with the *fear of disapproval, of criticism, of blame, or of accountability*. Furthermore, since Aaron's wife doesn't shy away from fully expressing her opinions and anger when things don't go her way, by complying with her wishes Aaron doesn't have to deal with the unpleasant consequences of upsetting her.

Because over the years Aaron has never had to take responsibility for anything, he's begun to doubt whether he can do so at all. He *fears making a wrong decision, being judged,* and ultimately *being exposed* for the Aaron that he believes he is: a weak, unconfident, and incapable man. Deep down, he believes his wife is smarter, more skilled, and more accomplished than he is. His deepest fear is exposure. If he makes the wrong decision, not only will it expose his failings—in that she will see him for what he really is—but it will also likely cause her to lose all respect for him and leave. This is a risk he's simply not willing to take. In addition to all this, Aaron fears having to be independent and having to fend for himself. He's never done that before and wonders if he'll cope.

Zara's Fears

As a child, Zara had a difficult time at school. The other children picked on her for being overweight and taunted her for being different. She would cry easily, and this made the bullying worse. Zara often felt isolated, anxious, and alone. She quickly learnt to be as quiet and inconspicuous as possible so as not to attract attention to herself. While this self-protective strategy sometimes worked as a child, it became a habit that she carried into adulthood, and it soon began to work against her.

Zara *fears being ridiculed, shunned, or attacked.* Consequently, she finds it difficult to articulate her thoughts and feelings and generally keeps herself to herself. Her childhood experiences have also made it difficult for her to trust others, because most of the time she felt unsafe.

Zara developed the misguided belief that others should just know what she's thinking, how she feels, and what she needs without her having to explicitly say so. Her husband does his best, but many times he gets it terribly wrong. This makes Zara very angry. For example, one Saturday during the summer, Zara and her husband had planned to drive to the beach and spend the day there. On the morning of the trip, Zara woke up with a headache. She'd slept badly and felt tired and grumpy. Going to the beach and pretending to be cheerful and energetic was the last thing she felt like doing. Her husband noticed she was a little quiet and asked her if everything was okay, in response to which Zara merely shrugged and almost inaudibly replied, "Hmm." He tried again. "What's up?" Zara felt upset now and said, "Nothing," in an agitated voice. Zara's husband mumbled something about her moody behaviour and then continued with his preparations. This made Zara angry. She thought that her tone of voice should have alerted him to the fact that she didn't want to go to the beach and that he ought to have realized this without her having to say as much—especially since she'd been tossing and turning half the night. Half an hour later, Zara became so incensed by what she perceived to be his lack of insight and concern that she completely shut down and went back to bed. While sitting in her bedroom, she heard her husband packing the car and getting their by now very excited five-year-old son ready. To her this was yet more proof that her husband didn't care about her. She had not been clear. He had not picked up on her clues and responded in the way she wanted him to by cancelling the trip. Zara would now have to face a confused and angry husband, and a disappointed and upset little boy.

Zara's habitual closed-off mode of relating to others stems from her inability to articulate her emotions—especially her anger, which simply builds up and gets the better of her. Deep down, Zara is frightened to say what she really thinks and wants from her husband because she's *frightened of rejection*. She's terrified that he will ignore her and her wishes. Over time, she's also become *fearful of her own anger*. Unsure how to deal with it, Zara continues to do the only thing she knows: suppress it and remain quiet.

Sharon's Fears

Sharon's unhealthy fears and beliefs have their roots in childhood as well. Having had a turbulent upbringing, Sharon learnt early on that it was safer for her to do as she was told and remain hidden from view. Her experiences with her alcoholic father and mentally ill mother taught her to equate any behaviour that attracted attention to her with danger. She also learnt that to stay out of trouble she must be fully obedient at all times.

She vividly remembers a time when, as a young child, she asked her mother if she would buy her a doll for her birthday. She was just about to show her the one she liked in a magazine when her drunken father came up behind her and slapped her hard on the head. "Doll! What do you want a doll for, you stupid child?!" he roared. "Don't you know we don't have any money for pointless things like that? When are you going to grow up? You idiot!" Zara felt crushed and very frightened.

Sharon's mother suffered from bipolar disorder and was equally unpredictable. During one particularly severe manic episode, she dragged Sharon down the street to the local store, refusing to let go of her hand or slow down despite her screams, merely because Sharon had dared to ask for sweets. On that occasion, Sharon experienced severe cuts and bruises to both her knees.

The volatile behaviour that both her parents displayed at times taught Sharon from a very young age that expressing her desires could be dangerous and result in verbal, emotional, and physical abuse. The fears underpinning Sharon's passive behaviour therefore include *the fear of offending others, the fear of being rejected*, and *the fear of being disapproved of.* Her experiences have taught her to be quiet and compliant. She deeply *fears being hurt if she upsets others by not doing what they want, and she fears being abused*. It took Sharon a long time to recover from her knee injuries; she vividly remembers the weeks of pain she had to endure. Sharon also *fears disappointment*. The painful feelings she experienced when as a little girl she didn't get the doll she so desperately wanted are still as real and intense for her now as they were then.

Sharon's childhood experiences have severely undermined her self-esteem. As is often the case with children who have not received emotional nurturing, Sharon internalized the belief that she was unlovable and that there must be something fundamentally wrong with her. As she grew into adulthood, this belief drove Sharon to constantly seek approval from others, be overly accommodating of others' needs, and engage in incessant people-pleasing behaviour. She's now *afraid of being disliked, letting others down*, and *being seen as unkind or difficult*. Sharon tries hard to form and maintain friendships by doing whatever it takes to keep her connections real and alive, because at some level she's convinced she isn't worthy of anyone's attention. Her *fear of being ostracized* is rooted in her *fear of being alone and not being able to cope*. She also holds a core fear that she is unsafe. This fear manifests in her life as self-protective behaviours, such as the perpetual people pleasing. Deep down, Sharon believes that if she always does what other people want her to do, they will not hurt her.

We all want to be accepted and to have positive connections with the people in our lives. It is for this reason that the greatest impediment to speaking our truth ultimately lies in the *fear of loss*: loss of face, loss of positive regard, loss of approval, loss of love, loss of control, and loss of relationships. This, coupled with the possible emotional repercussions (anxiety, shame, fear, guilt, and despair), acts as a powerful barrier to speaking our truth.

Self-Reflection Exercise 5: Uncovering Your Hidden Fears and Beliefs

It's now time for some self-reflection. What underlying fears prevent you from speaking your truth? Did any of the fears we've discussed here resonate with you?

Our thoughts and beliefs have such a profound influence on our feelings and behaviour, yet most of us rarely pay attention to the dialogue that goes on inside our heads. One of the most powerful ways to pinpoint your innermost beliefs is through journaling. Writing down your thoughts and feelings opens you up to, and sheds light on, your internal dialogue—something that is difficult to do by merely thinking about an issue. Journaling not only allows you to gain powerful personal insights into any issue but also allows you to access and uncover new and deeper layers of your psyche.

Here's an exercise you can do to uncover the beliefs that are holding you in a pattern of passive behaviour: You're going to do some focused work and dig deep inside yourself to find out what it is that you really fear—and therefore believe—when it comes to speaking up for yourself. You may find yourself feeling uncomfortable as you do this exercise, but keep in mind that you're working only in the realms of your imagination and that the purpose of this exercise is for you to gain clarity. You can only take steps to address your fears and unhelpful beliefs if you first know what they are. We will deal with the issues that come up as a result of this exercise in the next chapter, but for now, you need to start by establishing what your specific fearful or limiting beliefs are.

1. Carve out about half an hour of quiet time—a time when you're feeling relaxed and won't be disturbed. You'll need a pen and some paper or a journal.
2. Think about a *situation* in which you struggle to speak your truth. For the purposes of this exercise, the harder you find it to be assertive in this situation, the better.
3. Start by writing down everything you know about the situation, all the facts, in as much detail as possible. What is the situation? Who's involved? What's the specific scenario in which you struggle to express yourself honestly and confidently?
4. Identify a single truth that you would like to tell the person or people involved. What do you want to say? Write down the actual statement.
5. Now ask yourself, *What would happen if I said this?* For this part of the exercise, it's essential that you write down the first thing that comes to mind. Don't dwell on the answers or try to craft or censor them in any way. Just write down whatever comes to mind in whatever way it appears. The trick is to capture the essence of your initial response without giving your mind time to hinder or distort the message in any way.
6. Now ask yourself, *What would happen if this were to occur (your response to point 5)?*
7. Continue asking yourself this same question repeatedly in response to each answer you come up with: *And then what would happen?* Asking and answering these questions in quick succession will allow you to tap into your deepest fears.
8. Continue going deeper and deeper into each of the responses your mind offers up. Don't think about what you're writing

or censor it in any way. Just continue to write until you have nothing left to add.
9. Now read over what you've written. You should have some idea of the underlying fears that are preventing you from being assertive.
10. Next, ask yourself, *What would I lose by being assertive in this situation?* After each answer, ask yourself, *What else?* Keep going until you run out of ideas.
11. Now ask yourself, *What would I gain? How would being assertive in this situation benefit me? How else?* Again, write down everything that comes to mind.
12. You will have written down a fair amount of dialogue by now if you've engaged with the repetitive questioning format suggested. When you have nothing more to write, look back over what you've written. You should be able to identify the negative thoughts and the fearful beliefs that underpin your passive behaviour.

Some Examples

To give you an idea of how this exercise works in practice, here's an excerpt from Jasmine's journal.

> What situation do I struggle with? I wish I were more assertive with my family—especially my mother-in-law. Sometimes I just want a day off so I can lounge around and just "be" ... not do anything. I never get to relax. There's always something I should be doing. It's the same, day after day after day.
>
> I find it hard to be the one who's responsible for cooking all the time. I hate cooking, but I have to get that freshly cooked meal on that table every

single day, no matter how I'm feeling or how many other things I've got on my plate. I come home from work, and that's the first thing my mind turns to—what will I cook today? I hate this. I hate it. I hate it! I feel under so much pressure. No one else gives the evening meal a second thought. They just show up at dinner time with no regard for the effort I've put in. How the hell did this end up being my responsibility? They just show up at the table, expecting the food to be there ... ready. They take me for granted. They all take me for granted. I wonder what would happen if I just didn't do it one day? That would serve them right.

I desperately want to tell everyone in the family that I want one day off from cooking every week. I don't think that's too much to ask. There are other people living in this house too, and they could take on the task just one day a week. I want to say, "I need someone else to cook the meals every Sunday so I can have a break."

What would happen if I said this? All hell would break loose! Mum [Jasmine's mother-in-law] would get really upset with me. She'd go mad! She'd think I was being disrespectful. She'd say, "Who on earth do you think you are?!" I should know my place in the family. It's my responsibility to cook the evening meal. I'm the daughter-in-law; It's what daughters-in-law do—they cook for their families. It's what daughters-in-law have always done. It's their job. Who am I to say I don't want to do it? If I'm allowed to get away with not cooking one day a week, what other things will I suddenly start demanding?! Am I not going to clean? Am I not going to shop?

What would happen then? I might lose my temper and mouth off at her.

What would happen then? I'd feel so ashamed. It's wrong to talk back to your elders.

What would happen then? I'd lose the respect of everyone in the family. I'd feel bad about myself. I'd have let everyone down. I've worked so hard to gain everyone's respect, and I'll lose it all in one go.

What would happen then? Mum would complain to my parents.

What would happen then? My parents would be so upset with me. They'd collude with her and probably give me a real going-over … they'd give me an earful. I bet they'd all gang up on me. I don't think they'd see it from my point of view. I don't think anybody would take my side.

What would happen then? I'd be isolated. All alone.

What would happen then? I'd have no one. Tony probably wouldn't side with me either because I'd have upset so many people—especially his parents.

What would happen then? I'd lose everyone's love and respect. They'd turn me out.

What would happen then? I'd be all alone.

What would happen then? I couldn't cope.

What would happen then? I'd lose everything: my family, my husband, my kids.

What would happen then? I'd have let my kids down.

What would happen then? I'd have a breakdown. I'm nothing without my kids and family.

What would I lose by asking for one day off a week? Everything. I'd lose the love and regard of

> the most important people in my life: my kids and husband. I'd lose the approval of the people I love the most—especially my parents. I'd feel ashamed; they wouldn't approve of my behaviour. I know they wouldn't. I just know it.
>
> What would I gain? I'd have one day a week when I could relax and not have to worry about cooking everyone's dinner. I'd have one day a week when someone would do something for me instead of me doing everything for everyone else. I'd get some time to myself to maybe do something that I enjoy doing … or to just rest. I'm so tired.

Jasmine's journaling exercise has uncovered a fascinating range of fears and beliefs. Underneath it all, she's convinced that she knows exactly how her mother-in-law, her parents, her husband, and even her young children are going to react. She's worried about her own emotional reaction and losing control of herself. She's worried that she can't handle other people disapproving of her. And she has a clear, catastrophic picture in her mind about the likely outcome of her simple request: she would have a complete mental and emotional breakdown. This seems like a colossal price to pay for a little time out on a Sunday!

It's not difficult to see how Jasmine's beliefs are keeping her tightly locked into her passive behaviour. In her mind, there is no way out; the consequences of being assertive are enormous. This leaves her feeling trapped, petrified, and powerless.

We will be addressing these fears in the next chapter, but let's also take a look at Aaron's journal.

> What situation do I struggle with? I've really got to get my act together with Mia. I don't have a say in anything: where I go, what I do, what I eat—not

even what I wear. It shouldn't be like this. I'm the man; I should have some say in my own life! I do everything to keep her sweet, to please her, and to always let her have her own way, and even then I don't get a say in any of the decisions around here. It's not right. It shouldn't be like this. It just shouldn't.

It's not like that for everyone else. It's just me. My friends' wives don't behave like Mia. My friends don't have to put up with someone telling them what they should and shouldn't be doing all the time. It's not right. I can't put up with this any more.

I need to tell Mia that I want to visit my brothers and sisters whenever I want, and especially when they invite me over. I want to say, "Mia, Adam's invited me over for a beer, so I'm going round his on Friday night."

What would happen if I said this? She would flip out. She'd ask me why I want to waste my time going over there and what I want to go drinking with Adam for, saying he's a bad influence. She'd start going on about what a loser Adam is. She'd do what she always does and start putting him down. "Why doesn't he get a job ... Why does he always look so scruffy ... Why is his house such a mess ... Why doesn't he behave like an adult ... When's he going to grow up?" Blah, blah, blah. I'm so sick of it!

What would happen then? I'd just start tuning out, because I wouldn't be able to take it. Adam's a good guy; he's my brother. She's got him all wrong. He's none of the things she says he is. She doesn't even know him.

What would happen then? She'd notice I was not listening.

What would happen then? She'd start in on me, saying I need to grow up and need to stop wasting my life, and telling me I need to hang around with people who are worth hanging around with—people who are going somewhere. Blah, blah, blah. I don't even know what she's talking about half the time. She really annoys me. She really gets me down going on like that all the time.

What would happen then? She'd start laying into me and telling me I'm not responsible and not ambitious enough. She'd go on about buying a bigger house, how I need to get a better-paying job, how I don't listen to her, and how she's the one who's carrying me through life.

What would happen then? I'd get upset. I hate it when she's laying into me. I hate it when she shouts—when she tells me that I don't have any dreams, that I'm lazy, that I'm not trying hard enough, or that I'm a waste of space. It makes me feel so small.

What would happen then? I'd get angry and start arguing back.

What would happen then? She'd get even louder and more aggressive.

What would happen then? I might lose control of myself.

What would happen then? Oh my goodness! I can't even go there!

What would I lose by saying I'm going over to Adam's? My whole life as I know it. My sanity! She'd make my life a nightmare. I can't deal with all the shouting and screaming. She's crazy when she gets like that. It's bad enough having her badmouth my family, but then she'll just turn on me, saying I'm a loser, I should be more focused on our future, I should be this, and I should be that. Someday she's going to figure out she married the wrong man. She's going to realize I'm not the person she should be with. I'm not good enough for her and her fancy dreams. She'll just walk. She'll find her perfect high-flier and be off. And if I'm not careful, it won't be long before that happens. I'll lose everything. Everything.

What would I gain by saying I'm going over to Adam's? I'd get to spend time with my brother. I miss him. I miss his company. I can be myself with him. I'd get to do what I want for a change. I'd get to have some control over my life. I'd get to make my own decisions. I'd feel better about myself, like I have some power in this relationship, and like I'm important in some way. I'd feel that what I want matters and that she understands that.

Again, it's not difficult to see why Aaron chooses to remain quiet and subservient. In his mind, the repercussions of speaking up are simply too dire. He believes there's a risk he will draw his wife's attention to his shortcomings, and as soon as she realizes who he really is, she'll leave him. He'll be exposed for the fraud he imagines himself to be and, as a result, lose everything.

Your own journaling exercise will help you to identify some of the beliefs you are holding—beliefs that are keeping you stuck in your passive behaviour. You may highlight fears, worries, negative thoughts, excuses, justifications, conditioning from your family, personality traits such as perfectionism, and maybe even past experiences and failed attempts at being assertive.

Unhelpful Negative Thought Patterns

When we become more aware of our thoughts and hidden beliefs, we can also start to see that our perception of reality is affected by *how* we think. There are certain ways of thinking that lead to a misrepresentation of reality. David Burns, an eminent American psychiatrist, suggests that there are ten common ways in which a person can distort his or her thinking, all of which result in an overly negative perspective.[5] Looking over the writing exercise you've just done, can you identify any of these thought patterns in yourself?

1. **All-or-nothing thinking** occurs when you see things in black-and-white terms. If your performance falls short of perfect, you see yourself as a total failure.
2. **Overgeneralisation** occurs when you view a single negative event as a never-ending pattern of defeat.
3. **Mental filtering** occurs when you dwell on the negatives in a situation or person and ignore the positives.
4. **Discounting the positives** occurs when you reject positive experiences by insisting for one reason or another that they "don't count". You maintain a negative belief that is contrary to your everyday experiences.
5. **Jumping to conclusions** occurs when you interpret an event or situation negatively even though the facts do not convincingly support your conclusion. This can include (a) mind reading, in which you assume you know what the other person is thinking, and (b) fortune telling, in which you

---

[5] Burns, D. D., *Feeling Good: The New Mood Therapy*, HarperCollins Publishers, New York, 2009.

anticipate that things will turn out badly and are convinced that your prediction is an already-established fact.
6. **Magnification or minimisation** occurs when you exaggerate the importance of certain things or inappropriately discount their significance until they appear inconsequential.
7. **Emotional reasoning** occurs when you assume that your negative emotions necessarily reflect the way things really are: "I feel like an idiot, so I really must be one."
8. **"Should" statements** are made when you try to motivate yourself with "shoulds" and "shouldn'ts", as though you must be coerced and punished before you can be expected to do anything. "Musts" and "oughts" are also common offenders.
9. **Labelling and mislabelling** occurs when you identify your shortcomings and, instead of saying, "I made a mistake," tell yourself, "I'm a complete loser."
10. **Personalisation** occurs when you see yourself as the cause of some negative external event for which you were not primarily responsible, or when you blame others and overlook the ways in which your own attitude and behaviour may have contributed to a problem.

Our mindsets, habitual ways of thinking, and beliefs construct our day-to-day reality and strongly influence our behaviour. Very rarely do we turn the spotlight on our beliefs to assess whether they are either a help or a hindrance, or whether they are true or false. The journaling exercise you have done will help you to identify the beliefs you are holding that are inhibiting change. This is the first step. You can only consciously overcome these hindrances if you bring them out from the shadows of your mind into the clear light of your vision. Once you've identified your latent fears, you can then move on to the next step, which is to decide whether these fears have any substance.

6
Chapter

Overcoming Your Fears and Changing Your Unhealthy Beliefs

We've seen how powerful our underlying fears can be in locking us into passive behaviour. If you completed the exercise in chapter 5, you should have a good insight into the kinds of fears that are holding you back from asserting yourself. The next step is to tackle these fears. But first I must clarify the precise nature of the fear we're talking about here. In this chapter, we will be primarily interested in the word "FEAR" as an acronym for "false evidence appearing real". When you start to *analyse and unravel your fears, the power* they hold over you *begins to fade away*.

We all know that fear is very real and that it arises whenever we're faced with a danger or threat. Fear is a powerful and necessary survival mechanism that we all possess, and its purpose is to keep us safe and alive. For example, if you were to suddenly come face-to-face with a vicious dog, your fear would first alert you to the fact that there is danger in your immediate surroundings, and secondly it would trigger physiological changes in your body that are designed to help you either fight the threat or run away from it (the flight response).[6] This type of fear response is not only helpful; it is healthy and necessary. There is, however, a different kind of fear that can trigger the same physiological response but is not generated by real threats in our environment; it is fear that arises from the way we think about things. It is self-generated. This kind of fear surfaces in response to a *perceived* threat that has little or no substance to it.

My younger life was plagued by this type of fear, and for many years I struggled with the difficult thoughts and feelings that ensued. I know from first-hand experience how powerful, real, and debilitating this fear can feel. For me it became all-consuming; it seriously restricted my life in so many ways. It stopped me going out. It stopped me travelling on public transport. It stopped me exploring new interests and activities that I might have enjoyed. It caused me immense distress and suffering in the form of panic attacks and generalized anxiety disorder.

But then, with the help of a therapist, I began to closely scrutinize my fear. As I started to explore and analyse it, I soon discovered that it wasn't real in the same way that the fear triggered by a confrontation with a vicious dog is, even though it felt exactly the same. I realized that the fear I was dealing with stemmed from the way I was thinking about life. It was driven by factors that resided within me: my negative, unhealthy thoughts and beliefs. So, for example, I became aware that when I had a headache, it wasn't suddenly an ominous sign that I had a serious illness. Before this point, I was a hypochondriac. Any physical discomfort would trigger a cascade of negative thoughts which would culminate in vivid images of me being admitted into hospital—something that filled me with absolute dread.

---

[6] Cannon, W., *The Wisdom of the Body*, W.W. Norton & Company Inc., New York, 1963.

I also recall that when I was an undergraduate student, whenever I had a number of assignments to hand in by a specific deadline, I'd feel immense pressure and start to doubt my ability to get the work done. My negative thoughts would spiral out of control, and I'd end up panicking. I wasn't in any danger. There was no possibility of anything terrible happening to me. It was all in my mind. It was only later, as I worked with my therapist, that I came to understand that all these fears consisted of false evidence appearing real. I realized that I was creating this inner turmoil purely by the way I was thinking. And it didn't take me long to come to the conclusion that this was, in fact, good news.

The good news here is that if we ourselves create fear in our conscious or unconscious minds, then we also have the power to change it—and to ultimately eradicate it. That's an empowering realization! This is the process we're going to embark upon in this chapter. We're going to begin by directly challenging some of the fears that are very likely preventing you from being assertive. But before we do that, we need to talk about the concepts of emotional responsibility and self-care.

To change anything about yourself, you must first take ownership of your thinking, your emotions, and your behaviour. You must accept that your thoughts, feelings, and behaviours *belong to you*. You can no longer blame others or unfortunate life events for making you behave passively. If you accept this basic premise, you will soon realize that this is actually a liberating stance to take, because it means that no one else can control you. And if that's the case, then you, and you alone, have the power to change how you respond in any given situation.

My therapist, for example, would continually ask me what would happen if I didn't submit a piece of work on time. Would I really be thrown out of university? Was it really going to be the end of the world? She would also ask me what would happen if I didn't submit a perfect piece of work? (We'd identified my perfectionist attitude as an issue that needed to be addressed.) Surely a healthier expectation was to hand in an essay that was good enough to pass. What did a perfect essay look like anyway? No one was asking for perfection. This was a requirement I had imposed on myself, and it was one example of how my own outrageously high standards were causing me stress and anxiety. I grew to learn that it was my own thoughts that were causing the difficult feelings I was experiencing. I was indeed tormenting myself.

An added advantage of taking emotional responsibility for yourself in this way is that you can then allow others to take emotional responsibility for themselves. It leads to a natural acceptance that you cannot directly influence another person's thoughts, feelings, and behaviours. The responsibility for that lies with them. Therefore, if someone feels hurt because of your decision to be assertive, then that is something he or she has chosen to do, at some level. You haven't done it to that person; that person has done it to himself or herself.

Of course, being emotionally responsible does not mean that you can become belligerent, dismissive, or insensitive to others' needs and do and say whatever you please with little regard for other people's feelings. We know from Jasmine's journal, for instance, that she feels under pressure to manage her many responsibilities at home and at work. In her case, being assertive does not mean that she simply refuses to do all the things she does around the house, ignoring or dismissing the effect this will have on the people living with her. That would be a misapplication of this principle. You may recall that in chapter 1 we established that the principle of equality and being mindful of the delicate balance of power between you and others sits right at the heart of being assertive. This is a good time to gain clarity about that balance of power, particularly regarding self-care and respect for others. Being emotionally responsible is about being aware of and owning your feelings while at the same time being conscious of how you're relating to other people and respecting their right to their own feelings.

Self-care is the main motivational force behind the desire to be more assertive. This essentially means considering your own interests first. It means that in any given situation you start by giving serious attention and thought to your own preferences first. Now, on its own, self-care can easily turn into selfishness. That's why it's important that you temper self-care with regard for others.

Having respect for others means acknowledging that you live in a community with other people who have their own preferences and that you *must consider their needs appropriately and in equal measure to your own.* Your needs are neither superior nor inferior to the needs of others. This principle ensures that you remain flexible in your approach. There are going to be times when your needs cannot be met because another person's needs are more pressing or must be prioritized. For example, whose needs would you prioritize in the following situation? One evening, you decide to work late to meet a deadline. Your partner calls to inform you that a member of the family has been taken seriously ill. Your partner then asks you to come home to be with the children while he or she goes to the hospital. Would you stay at work in order to meet your deadline, or would you go home? I believe it would be reasonable in this situation for your partner's needs and his or her concern for your relative to take precedence over your work deadline. There will always be times in life when you'll have to consider other people's needs and arrive at a healthy compromise. If you keep the principles of both self-care and regard for others at the forefront of your mind, it's likely that you will successfully create change as you seek to become more assertive.

Dealing with the Common Fears and Beliefs that Inhibit Assertive Behaviour

Now let's look at the fears and beliefs that often come up as barriers to assertiveness. These can manifest in a variety of ways, but on closer inspection, it's evident that they all boil down to seven main concerns. In the sections that follow, we're going to look at each of them in turn and discuss how you can deal with them.

The Fear of Being Disliked

This fear is at the core of many people's passive behaviour. The unhealthy belief is as follows: *People won't like me if I don't agree with them and quietly comply with their wishes.* We all actively crave approval, warmth, and validation from others. These things make us feel accepted and safe within our family and community. However, this desire can easily become an unhealthy need, which in turn compels us to ignore the principle of self-care and instead focus on the principle of regard for others. Let's look at this fear in more detail.

Do you believe it's possible to be liked by absolutely everyone all of the time? How many people do you know that have achieved this status? I can tell you that I don't know anyone who has done so. In fact, even if we look at the greatest, most popular, most influential people who've ever walked on this planet, we soon discover that none of them enjoyed universal acceptance, no matter how exalted a status they had in their community while they lived or how their lives were subsequently recorded in the history books. Look at the lives of Jesus, Martin Luther King Jr, Nelson Mandela, and Mother Teresa. You can always find someone who disagreed with them or even despised them. The reason for this is that every human being has a different perspective: different likes and dislikes. What pleases one person will displease another. Therefore, to attempt to please everyone all the time is an impossible task; it is unrealistic, and it is unachievable. (You can see here how the unhealthy belief *Everyone should like me at all times* generates the fear of not being liked.)

It's nice to have other people approve of you, like you, and accept you, but you must be open to the realistic possibility that occasionally some people will dislike and disapprove of you. You need to arrive at a place within yourself where you acknowledge that you may *like the approval of others*, but you *don't need that approval to survive*. You will be all right without it.

So how do you let go of the need for approval? The first step is to strengthen your sense of self by acknowledging that just because a few people dislike you, that doesn't affect your inherent value as a person. The more you value, trust, and accept yourself, the less other people's opinions will affect you. The greater your self-worth, the less hold this fear will have over you. (We'll talk more about how to cultivate a healthy level of self-worth later on in this chapter.)

Secondly, be open to the idea that other people's reactions to you are more a reflection of their inner selves and their issues than they are about you. Just because someone disapproves of something you're doing doesn't automatically make him or her right and you wrong. It simply means that person holds a different view of how the world should be. This doesn't automatically mean your view or stance is somehow less valid than that of the other person.

Thirdly, reflect on the issue of personal power. How, when, and why did you hand over your power to the person whose approval you're seeking? What makes that person's opinion of you so important?

Fourthly, consider the real—not imagined—consequences of the other person's disapproval of you. How will this impact your everyday life? Be honest with yourself. What difference will it really make to you? You'll probably find that, other than bringing up some negative feelings, it has little impact.

And, lastly, move to a greater understanding and acceptance of the fact that you can't control another person's reactions. This goes back to the issue of emotional responsibility we discussed earlier. We can only ever control our own reactions. If someone wants to dislike or disapprove of you, then that is his or her choice and right. It doesn't have to hurt or bother you. If it does, it's because you are choosing to allow it to do so.

The Fear of Being Rejected

We humans are social creatures. Our lives depend on other people. These connections not only bring us happiness; they are crucial to our survival. We're all biologically hard-wired to want to be part of a community, and we crave a sense of belonging and acceptance. After all, there is safety in numbers. It is not difficult to imagine a time when our ancestors had to contend with predators and the fear of starvation. Being a member of a group meant they could collaborate and defend each other. Being ostracized from that group significantly reduced their chances of survival; it could literally result in death. It's not surprising, therefore, that the thought of being rejected by our social group fills us with horror and induces feelings of fear and anxiety.

Rejection can mean being expelled from the group altogether, but it can also be more subtle than that; it can mean having our views, thoughts, or ideas dismissed or ridiculed by others in the group. We can see, then, why the fear of rejection can be a major obstacle on the road to assertiveness. It's easy to conclude that conforming and complying with other people's wishes will minimize the risk of rejection and maximize the chances of acceptance. So here's the unhealthy belief—and it serves to create a false sense of safety.

When looking at the fear of rejection, two issues need to be addressed: (1) the catastrophic thoughts that often accompany deep-rooted fears, and (2) your own tolerance threshold for coping with rejection.

Left unchecked and unscrutinised, fears tend to unconsciously drive irrational thinking and behaviour. Conversely, when you analyse your fears, you often find there's little substance to them. Let's consider whether assertiveness really carries the risk of rejection.

If you express your preferences politely and respectfully in any given situation while at the same time being mindful of other people's preferences, are you really going to be rejected, shamed, and disowned? Would this happen in reality? Think about it for a moment. Would you really end up as a social outcast?

The mind can easily engage in catastrophic thinking, in which it views things in "all-or-nothing" terms. But life is rarely that black and white. Yes, people may be surprised that you've stated an opinion when you usually refrain from doing so, or they may disapprove of, and even condemn, you for speaking up; but are they likely to completely reject you and the role you play in their life? It's highly unlikely. And here's why.

The fear that you'd become a pariah if you ever dared to speak up ignores the mutual dependency of most of your relationships. The truth is that people need you in their lives just as much as you need them. This fear has its roots in, and reflects, your own insecurities, because it is your own lack of self-worth that feeds it. If at some level you believe you're not important enough for other people to accommodate your needs and desires, or that people tolerate you only because you comply all the time, you're going to avoid being assertive, because the fear of rejection is petrifying.

The second issue to consider when it comes to the fear of rejection is your ability to tolerate different degrees of rejection. Can you tolerate negative attention? Can you tolerate disapproval? Can you tolerate criticism? No one likes to be on the receiving end of this kind of behaviour; it makes us feel bad. But when you're subjected to it, can you cope? How do you react? Are you completely thrown off balance and unable to function, or do you feel down but then bounce back fairly quickly? It's important to develop some tolerance to rejection simply because it is, to a lesser or greater extent, an inevitable part of life. The reality is that when you move from being passive to being assertive, it is highly likely you will experience rejection from some people. It's important to realize that being rejected does not make you worthless; it's simply another person's perspective on how things should be.

If you feel the fear of rejection is holding you back, there are two things you can do. Firstly, you can take steps to ascertain exactly how much rejection you're able to handle. You can do this by deliberately putting yourself in situations where you're increasingly exposed to a greater degree of rejection so you can assess how you react. For example, when you're with a group of people, you might try expressing an opinion that you know others will disagree with and then observe your internal response. A negative reaction from your audience is likely to cause some emotional, and perhaps even physical, discomfort. Expect this to happen. But also remember that these feelings and sensations will soon pass. Just focus on breathing deeply and stay in the moment. Afterwards, reflect on how your reaction compared to what you thought you'd feel and do. Your mind can sometimes fool you into expecting things to be much worse than they are.

Secondly, as you expose yourself to little bouts of rejection in this way, over time you'll begin to build up a resistance to it. Your tolerance threshold will begin to rise, and you'll find that you can tolerate the bad feelings, should you need to do so. This way, the unhealthy belief *I need to do what others want all the time so that I won't be rejected* gradually transforms into the more positive belief *It's safe for me to say what I think, and I can cope if this sometimes means I'm rejected.*

Rejection is unpleasant. It's an uncomfortable feeling, and nobody likes it. However, if you want to live a full life, you're not going to be immune to it. It's rarely the end of the world, and although it can be difficult to stomach, you can handle it.

The Fear of Being Selfish

Many of us, because of our upbringing, fear that other people will see us as selfish. This thought fills us with dread. We don't want others to think we're selfish, and we don't want to perceive ourselves as selfish either. Most of us have successfully internalized the message that being selfish is immoral; we believe it is wrong and unacceptable. And indeed it is. The problem, however, is that many people hold back from being assertive because they **wrongly confuse assertive behaviour with selfishness.** They have the unhealthy belief *It's selfish to assert my needs and wishes, and being selfish is wrong.*

The fear of being selfish often drives people to the opposite end of the behaviour spectrum, where they completely neglect themselves. This means that they ignore their own interests and consistently put others' interests first. We've already established that assertive behaviour demands a balance of power between ourselves and the people in our lives. Selfishness and self-neglect are both imbalanced behaviours. A selfish attitude puts your needs above those of others, and a self-neglecting attitude puts others' needs above your own. Assertiveness is neither of these. The healthy belief underpinning assertiveness is that everyone's needs are important and worthy of consideration. This includes your own.

Opting for self-neglecting behaviour as a result of the misguided belief that it's the only alternative to selfish behaviour leads to passiveness, the consequences of which we explored in chapter 3. Self-neglecting behaviour does not earn you respect. In fact, it does the opposite: it sends out a clear and loud message to others that you don't matter. And then you soon find that people ignore your wishes and needs, take you for granted, and even disrespect you. What they're doing is holding up a mirror to the way you're treating yourself.

Ultimately this fear hinges on the relationship you have with yourself. It's about your sense of self-worth and how much self-love you have. Are you important in your own eyes, or are you worthless? To have self-worth is to know that you have an inherent value simply because you exist. It's about who you are, not what you do. It's about the unique qualities that make you, you. Behind the fear of being selfish sits the unhealthy belief *I'm not important or of value.* So developing a sense of self-worth is essentially about changing that belief to a healthier, more self-affirming one. We'll talk about how to do that later in this chapter.

Cultivating a healthy sense of self-worth is of vital importance, because your level of self-worth dictates the quality of your entire existence. It determines how you conduct yourself in your day-to-day life and how you allow others to treat you. Self-worth is simply a consequence of believing that you are worthy. The only person who ultimately decides how important you are in your world is you.

To overcome the fear of being selfish, you must cultivate a strong belief in your own worth. You must believe that you are at least of equal worth to everyone else in your life. Yes, we're all different; we have different strengths and weaknesses, but these do not make us inferior or superior to others. When you have wholeheartedly adopted this belief, you will be neither selfish nor self-neglecting. You will occupy the healthy middle ground, where you value and consider everyone's needs and wishes, including your own.

The Fear of Hurting or Upsetting Others

Of all the fears we've looked at so far, it is the fear of hurting or upsetting others that is most likely to halt your attempts at being assertive. As well as being a major obstacle to assertiveness, it also keeps people trapped in unhealthy relationships.

Picture this: One day you decide to tell your housemate that she needs to start pulling her weight around the house. You calmly draw her attention to the fact that she never tidies up after herself, rarely puts the rubbish out, and leaves dishes in the sink for you to wash almost every day. However, the minute you've uttered these words, she looks visibly upset: tears well up in her eyes, and she starts to cry gently. She makes it absolutely clear that she's hurt by what you've said. What's the natural thing for you to do in that instance? Retreat straight back into being quiet and meek, of course. Most of us would avoid deliberately hurting another human being. We instinctively feel bad when someone is upset by our words or actions, both for them and about ourselves. It damages our sense of self. So the unhealthy belief here is that *I'm a bad person if I say or do something that upsets another person.*

But if you stop and reflect on what's really going on, you'll soon realize that the people who are alarmed at your assertive behaviour are using *their reactions* to *control and manipulate you*. And the reason is that they very likely have a vested interest in ensuring that you remain submissive—so much so that if you dare to challenge them or state an opinion they don't like, they pull out their trump card: you're a bad person. You're selfish, disrespectful, and have no regard for anyone else's feelings. This reaction has one sole aim, and that is to make you feel guilty and ashamed. Both these emotions are so powerful that they will stop most of us in our tracks. The only way to deal with this situation is to see through the manipulation that is at work here.

Let's go back to the principle of emotional responsibility. Can you really make someone react in a certain way completely against his or her will? If someone has chosen to be unhappy, do you have the power to make him or her happy? I don't think so. None of us are so powerful that we can fully control another person's feelings, thoughts, or actions. That power lies within the other person. There are some obvious exceptions (hurting others through violence, for example), but generally speaking, you do not have the power to make someone feel hurt and upset. At some level, the other person is choosing to respond in that way. And that is his or her choice. It has nothing to do with you. Remember, the *responsibility* for the *response* lies with the *responder*. If you accept this principle, then the fear of hurting and upsetting others will gradually diminish. As you take full responsibility for yourself, you will leave others to take full responsibility for themselves. If you notice that there are people in your life who refuse to take responsibility in this way and want to blame you for all their reactions, then you will have to decide whether you're going to continue to tolerate their conscious or unconscious manipulation.

We've already established that being assertive is about considering other people's needs as well as your own. If you're mindful of others' thoughts and feelings, are polite and respectful in the way you communicate your own needs and wishes, and are clear that your desire to be more assertive is not driven by a wish to cause deliberate hurt and pain, then experience will soon show you that your fear of hurting others is grossly exaggerated. People will not behave in the way that you feared. Furthermore, if people in your life are initially a little taken aback because you've found your voice, you can feel safe in the knowledge that (a) hurting them was never your intention, (b) they are responsible for their reactions, and (c) they, and you, can handle any temporary discomfort that may occur as you move into this new way of behaving. So, looping back to the unhealthy belief we started with, a more positive belief is *If other people have a negative reaction to what I say, it doesn't mean I'm wrong or a bad person.*

You may have been in unhealthy relationships, ones in which the power dynamics are unbalanced, for a long time. If that's the case, know that sometimes, in the short term, your attempts to assert yourself may occasion some mild distress in another person. It's essential that you learn to tolerate this if you're ever going to make things better for yourself—and the other person—in the long term.

The Belief that Others Know What We Want

For some people, a major obstacle to speaking up and clearly expressing their thoughts, feelings, needs, and desires is the irrational belief that others should know what they want simply from their body language, tone of voice, or prior knowledge of them as a person. How many people do you know that are able to read your mind? I don't know any! Nobody knows how you feel or what you want, no matter how well he or she knows you, unless you clearly tell that person.

The erroneous belief that others should know how you feel and what you want thwarts assertive behaviour in two specific ways. In the first instance, it encourages you to behave passively. It causes you to stay in your comfort zone and not speak up, because you falsely assume that others already know your thoughts and feelings. Secondly, it encourages aggressive behaviour, which can either be overt or manifest as passive aggression. Examples of passive-aggressive behaviour can include insisting you're all right when you are clearly angry or upset; verbally shutting down and refusing to articulate your true thoughts and feelings; taking on tasks and then deliberating on choosing to not complete them; intentionally causing confusion around an issue, such as where and when you intend to meet someone; sulking; and being obstructive. Passive-aggressive behaviour puts the other person in a no-win situation. They struggle to understand your needs and thus can't take appropriate action to help you get those needs met. And when they don't notice your subtle hints about what you want, it's easy for you to interpret this negatively. The self-talk can go something like this: *They don't care. They're deliberately trying to wind me up. They don't think I'm important.*

When we expect people to behave in a certain way and they don't, it's easy to jump to conclusions that aren't based in reality. We can easily make negative assumptions about what the other person's behaviour means without really knowing what's going on inside him or her. This kind of misguided and negative self-talk does little for a person's self-esteem; not only can it catapult a person into a bad mood, but if experienced regularly, it can even warp a person's personality. This is what has happened to Zara. In chapter 3, we looked at how Zara's self-talk and tendency to shut down instead of relating to her husband in a positive way has caused her to become passive-aggressive. This is a toxic behaviour that is incredibly destructive to a person's relationships, health and well-being. Isn't it easier and more constructive to speak your truth in the first place and not let things escalate to sometimes irreparable proportions?

We can't read each other's minds accurately, if at all, so this irrational belief needs to be replaced with a healthier one, such as: *It would be nice for so and so to be so in tune with me that he [or she] knows how I feel, but he [or she] is not telepathic, so unless I communicate my thoughts and feelings to him [or her] clearly, he [or she] may not know.* And it's vital to then put this positive belief into practice. Learning to be assertive and to speak up when it matters is the only way to break the destructive behavioural cycle of passivity and passive-aggression.

The Belief that Life Should Be Easy and Trouble-Free

As with most things, you get out of life what you put into it. It can be easy to fall into the trap of thinking that life should always be plain sailing, and that issues should resolve themselves satisfactorily without you having to put in any effort or experience any discomfort. This belief can seriously hinder a person's attempts at moving from a place of passivity to a place of assertiveness.

If we demand that life be easy-going and devoid of problems, we're unlikely to have the personal resolve and commitment that's required to break the passivity cycle. At the very least, being assertive will require effort, but it's also likely to bring up some personal discomfort. If we're not ready to accept and tolerate that, we're likely to slip into the assumption that assertion is simply not worth all the aggravation. Our fallback position becomes one of avoiding confrontation at all costs, and we become locked in a vicious cycle: we're unhappy about our passive behaviour and its consequences; we consider changing; we want an easy, trouble-free life; we realize change requires effort; we decide that it's not worth the effort; we retreat to a place of passivity. Aaron, the thirty-seven-year-old IT consultant, takes this position. His easy-going, non-confrontational personality prevents him from addressing the power imbalance in his marriage. Despite feeling frustrated and unhappy, he's reluctant to stand up to his wife because it risks creating discord, and it is this that keeps him locked in a place of passivity.

At first learning to be assertive can induce feelings of awkwardness, discomfort, and fear. But, over time, these feelings subside as you begin to embed your new skills into your everyday life and adopt a new way of living. As discussed earlier, you may experience some resistance from those around you too, but again, this subsides in time as people get used to the new you.

It's natural to fear that people will react negatively if we start to express ourselves, but as with most fears, the problem can seem worse in our minds. As long as you apply the principles of assertiveness properly, respect other people's needs and wishes as well as your own, behave in a calm and relaxed way, and speak politely and respectfully, you may be pleasantly surprised to find that you don't get a negative reaction at all.

Addressing any unrealistic and unhelpful beliefs you hold around wanting an easy and effortless life is essential if you are to move from a place of passivity to assertion. A more productive belief would be *Yes, I want an easy life, but I know I'm not immune from difficulties and discomfort. If things do get uncomfortable, I can handle it.* Becoming more assertive will demand deliberate action and consistent effort and may initially cause some temporary discomfort, but the long-term benefits of making this extra effort will significantly outweigh the costs.

The Belief that It's Not Safe to Experience and Express Your Feelings

We live our lives primarily through our emotions. If you think about it, it's rarely what happens to you that's the issue; it's how you *feel* about it that really matters. We define a situation as good or bad based on our mental and emotional response. You can put two people in the same situation and find that they both respond to the same circumstances in different ways based on their personal preferences, which emanate, fundamentally, from their emotional reaction.

Our feelings are the communication system of our inner world. They carry important messages from the deeper parts of our being, often helping to bring to our conscious awareness the things we need to pay attention to in our inner and outer reality. Anger is a complex emotion, but one of its functions is to alert us to the fact that someone has violated our boundaries. Guilt draws our attention to something we believe we have done wrong. Sadness and despair signal that someone or something has hurt us and our capacity to cope has been severely diminished. We need to acknowledge, accept, and listen to all our emotional responses. I've come to realize that a life spent without honouring one's emotions is a life unlived. In everything we do, and in every moment of our lives, we are in a permanent state of experience. And the quality of that experience, whether it's wonderful or challenging, is defined by the way we feel.

Your emotions connect you to your deepest and most fundamental needs, to your yearnings and desires. They let you know when life is working for you, and they also tell you when something is wrong. Emotions help you to successfully steer yourself through life. After all, your most basic instincts prompt you to move towards things that make you feel good and away from things that make you feel bad. Therefore, when something inside you is crying out to be heard, you need to listen, and you need to respond.

A fully functioning human being not only acknowledges his or her feelings but also heeds and acts upon the messages that these feelings carry. He or she will pay attention to his or her emotional responses and allow his or her emotions to flow freely in and out of his or her body. For many people, however, there are times when life becomes so challenging that their emotions become too distressing for them to process in the moment; they cannot deal with the intensity of their feelings. This can happen, for example, when someone is young and lacks emotional maturity; when a person doesn't have enough time, energy, space, and support to work through their emotions; or when someone has been through a trauma. In these instances, to cope in the moment, a person may (a) disconnect from their emotional body and (b) continue to expend a considerable amount of conscious and unconscious energy on ignoring, suppressing and hiding these difficult feelings.

There's a tendency in our society to admire people who show resilience and fortitude in the face of adversity. This has led many people to internalize the belief that it's best to exercise restraint when it comes to expressing their emotions. There's a widely held belief that it's unwise to show too much, if any, emotion because it may be perceived as a personality flaw or a weakness. If you're one of these people, I would encourage you to rethink these views because, firstly, they have the potential to cause you mental and physical harm, and secondly, they will seriously hinder your attempts to become assertive.

If I could go back thirty years and give my younger self some advice, it would be "Stop avoiding your emotions." Back in those days, I spent a lot of energy suppressing my feelings. I tried hard to fit in, to do the right thing, and to avoid drama of any kind. I had emotional regulation down to a fine art. The world saw me as calm, quiet, and amiable, while deep inside there was turmoil and emotional chaos. It took me a long time to figure out that this strategy of avoiding my emotions was not serving me well. I may have been successful in pushing down difficult feelings at the time, but in the long term I paid a high price as far as my mental, emotional, and physical health were concerned.

Reflect on how you deal with unpleasant feelings. Think back to the last time you felt an intense emotion, such as anger, guilt, fear, or shame. Can you remember how you dealt with that emotion?

Did you allow yourself to fully experience the feeling? Or, like many people, did you find yourself trying to avoid it at all costs?

In the face of uncomfortable, painful, and traumatic feelings, we can all develop complex habits that help us to manage our distress and cope with life's demands. Here are some commonly used avoidance tactics.

- **Intellectualizing**: Intellectualizing occurs when you feel an emotion like anger, for example, but tell yourself that it's unjustified—that you're being silly and shouldn't feel this way, that you've misunderstood, or that you should know better than to react like this. It's when you think about what you're feeling and try to rationalize it away rather than experience it.
- **Denial**: Denial occurs when you choose to ignore the feeling completely. You don't allow yourself to dwell on it, or worse still, you don't even allow the thought that there are feelings you need to deal with to surface.
- **Suppression**: Suppression occurs when you deliberately push down a feeling as soon as it arises. Some people literally swallow in an attempt to hold down the unpleasant sensations. Other people purposely take a deep breath to regain their composure and move their attention away from the feeling.
- **Anesthetizing**: An example of anesthetizing is using substances, such as alcohol, drugs, or food, to numb troubling feelings.
- **Distraction**: You can become so busy that there's no time or space for your feelings to rise to the surface. Over-working and over-exercising are examples of distraction.
- **Rescuing**: Rescuing is another form of distraction. It occurs when you fill your mind, time, and life with other people's

problems, conveniently convincing yourself that their needs are more important and urgent than your own.
- **Emotional Disconnection:** Emotional disconnection is similar to intellectualizing in that you stay in your head. You overthink, analyse, and rationalize to such an extent that you never allow your conscious awareness to travel down into your body where your feelings reside.
- **Trivializing:** When you engage in trivializing, you consciously or unconsciously keep your interactions with others at a very superficial level. You never have in-depth conversations with anyone, choosing instead to focus on frivolous interactions and activities.
- **Pretence:** Pretence occurs when you wear a mask—a smile, for example—that hides your true feelings from the world. I was a master of this!

In fact, our society is rife with emotional suppression. Notice the number of times you are asked how you are by someone you know, causing you to feel duty-bound to reply, "I'm fine, thank you," maybe even with a big smile on your face. Deep down, you know that person is not really interested in how you are; he or she is just being polite. And on occasions, you likely said you were fine even though you weren't feeling fine at all.

There's no denying that life can be tough. We all shy away from experiencing difficult emotions. That's why we need to have an internal mechanism in place that enables us to regulate our emotions so we can function in the world with a degree of self-control. In the short term, avoiding our feelings every now and again doesn't do us any harm. However, doing this consistently over the long term can have a devastating impact on our well-being. Suppression is a dangerous thing. Here's why.

In their purest form, emotions are *energy* (e) in *motion*. This energy needs to flow—to move through your awareness. When you suppress it, all you do is bury it below the surface and then waste further precious energy holding it down there. The problem is that the energy is still there, bubbling away, waiting for expression. It doesn't just disappear. It's like a pressure cooker; the energy becomes increasingly intense until one day it erupts. That eruption might come in the form of a huge, aggressive outburst, a nervous breakdown, or a physical illness or disease. Symptoms of suppressed emotions can also include fatigue, anxiety, depression, constant irritability, bodily aches and pains, lack of motivation and drive, and a bitter, resentful attitude.

If you believe you're somewhat disconnected from your emotional body, here are some simple strategies you can use to help yourself to reconnect.

Paying attention

The first thing you must do is turn inwards and pay closer attention to the sensations that appear in your body. Thoughts reside in the mind. Emotions reside in the body. Get into the habit of regularly scanning your body with the intention of noticing your emotions.

Feelings Vocabulary

Secondly, improve your "feelings vocabulary". Many of us find it difficult to articulate how we feel simply because we cannot find the right words. There are many online resources that can help you get better at articulating your feelings. The Feeling Wheel, developed by Dr Gloria Willcox, is a particularly useful one.[7] It depicts six main human emotions and then elaborates on each one to show other linked emotions. You can use it to identify what it is that

---

[7] Willcox, G., "The Feeling Wheel: A Tool for Expanding Awareness of Emotions and Increasing Spontaneity and Intimacy", *The Transactional Analysis Journal*, 12/4 (1982), 274–76.

you're currently feeling, and then "drill down" further to discover associated feelings so you can understand your current state of mind and emotions in a deeper way. For example, if you're feeling scared, can you pinpoint whether you're also feeling confused, rejected, helpless, submissive, insecure, or anxious? If you're feeling peaceful, are you content, thoughtful, loving, thankful, or relaxed?

Journaling

Thirdly, give journaling a go. As we've touched on already, journaling is a highly effective tool for connecting with and managing the emotions. The practice of keeping a diary or journal, where you explore the thoughts and feelings that arise from situations and events in your life, can help you gain clarity and insight. If you've ever felt all tangled up inside and unsure of what you want or feel, taking a few minutes to jot down your thoughts and emotions will quickly put you in touch with your inner world. Journaling can also help you to discover and deal with feelings from the immediate, or even distant, past.

The joy of journaling is that it's a private and personal activity in which you can express yourself fully without the need for self-censorship. The process of writing not only connects you to your feelings but also helps you to release the emotions that are troubling you. It can be very helpful in processing your thoughts and stopping you from ruminating. It's also a highly effective way for you to get to know yourself better, manage stress, and problem-solve. Some people journal regularly, while others take time out to write down and explore their feelings only when intense emotions come up.

Talking

Another effective way to connect with your feelings is to talk to someone you trust about what's going on in your world and how you're experiencing life. This can be someone in your personal life who has no involvement in the issue you wish to discuss and is therefore neutral, or it could be a trained professional, such as a counsellor or life coach. Talking is very therapeutic. It can help you to sort through your thoughts, to identify and connect with your true feelings, and to find solutions to issues that trouble you. If you've chosen the right person to confide in, you'll find that talking will help you gain more self-awareness and a better understanding of yourself. If you commit to a process of self-enquiry and self-reflection, it will significantly enhance your ability to connect with your true self. It will improve your relationship with yourself, increase your confidence and self-esteem, and give you back your power. As you begin to better understand yourself, your intentions, your dreams, and your aspirations, you will naturally want to empower yourself to make positive changes that improve the quality of your life. Knowledge really is power; and there is no greater personal power than self-knowledge.

So far we've dealt with the first part of the belief that it's not safe to experience and express your feelings—the need to acknowledge and feel your emotions. The second part of this belief concerns your willingness to *express* your true feelings. You may be someone who's aware of your feelings but chooses not to articulate them to others, and it is this decision that acts as an internal barrier to asserting yourself. The choice to remain silent can be conscious or unconscious. The chances are that your unwillingness to fully express yourself is a learned childhood response. Somewhere along the line, your experiences have taught you to keep quiet. For example, if when you were young you spoke about your feelings and received a negative reaction, or even verbal or physical aggression, it makes perfect sense that you would then decide to keep your thoughts, feelings and preferences to yourself. It's natural for a child to quickly conclude that it's safer to be silent.

At one point in your life, this defence strategy probably served you well; it protected you from psychological, and perhaps even physical, harm. But now, in adulthood, you may find that it's getting in your way and preventing you from getting what you need and desire. If that's the case, you need to acknowledge and work through any unresolved traumatic or difficult experiences from your past. Journaling or talking things through with a trained professional can help you do this.

The belief that it's not safe to express one's feelings seriously hinders a person's ability to be assertive. If you recall, in chapter 1 we learnt that the key elements of assertiveness are

- connecting with your inner self;
- determining what your thoughts, feelings, and preferences are in any given situation;
- acknowledging the validity of these thoughts, feelings, and preferences;
- honestly communicating your thoughts, feelings, and preferences to others in a calm, respectful, firm way;
- choosing to communicate at a time that is appropriate; and
- not insisting that your preferences are the only ones that matter.

It's clear from this definition that your feelings are a crucial internal reference point when it comes to determining your preferences; and they're also a vital component of the overall information you need to communicate to others so they understand your position regarding any given situation.

It's virtually impossible for people to work out how you feel about something unless *you specifically and clearly tell them*. Communicating your feelings helps other people to understand you, your needs, and your preferences so that they can decide how to respond based on the actual information you've given them rather than on the assumptions they've made about how you feel. It's also key to forging positive connections with others, which is why assertiveness is the pathway to healthy relationships. As you express your true feelings to other people, they will sense that you are being genuine and authentic. It will encourage them to feel safe in doing the same with you, and in this way you will forge stronger connections with them.

Learning to be assertive will require that you pay attention to your feelings and that you overcome the urge to keep your feelings to yourself.

How to Cultivate Greater Self-Worth

The concept of self-worth has come up several times in this chapter, and that's because it underpins many of the unhealthy beliefs and fears we have explored. In this section, we're going to look at *how* you can nurture a more positive sense of self. Doing so will significantly enhance your ability and willingness to be assertive.

Improving your self-worth involves cultivating an attitude of optimism, positive expectation, and self-belief. It's about having positive self-regard. If you struggle with low self-esteem, there are steps you can take to address the issue.

Start by reflecting on how you treat yourself.

- Are you kind, compassionate, and mindful of your own needs?
- Are you generous towards yourself?
- Do you tolerate and accept the parts of yourself you don't like?
- When you've done something wrong, do you forgive yourself?
- Are you the opposite of all these things: mean, demanding, critical, unforgiving, and judgmental?

I'm often shocked by the harshness with which people treat themselves. Somehow, through their life experiences, many people have learnt that it's acceptable to condemn, belittle, and criticize themselves without the slightest degree of self-restraint. Ironically, very few of us would ever dream of being as obnoxious to another human being as we are to ourselves.

Once you've taken stock of where you are on the spectrum of self-acceptance, self-love, and self-worth, decide to change your attitude towards yourself.

Be Kind to Yourself

Take deliberate steps to treat yourself with more warmth, kindness, tolerance, and compassion. Learn to love and respect yourself. Be more accepting of yourself, warts and all. In particular, notice the times when your inner critic becomes loud, harsh, and judgmental, and choose to replace those thoughts with more caring and positive ones.

Notice Your Own Needs

Take time to reconnect with yourself by regularly monitoring what's going on inside your mind and your body. Start to notice your own needs, and then find ways to take better care of those needs. Be more honest with yourself about how you truly feel about the people and situations in your life.

Take Time Out for Yourself

Make time for yourself so that you have space to rest, reflect, and just *be* on a daily basis. This can be as uncomplicated as sitting quietly for fifteen minutes with a cup of tea, writing in a journal, soaking in a warm bath, or going for a walk by yourself. Ideally, you should establish a daily meditation practice. If you quieten down your mind, you will discover a beautiful, peaceful, joyful place within that you can access at any time, irrespective of what is going on in the world around you.

Connect with Your Creativity

Another powerful way to cultivate greater self-worth is by identifying creative activities that give you joy and devoting some time to them. Art, music, photography, writing, cooking, baking, and gardening are just a few examples. Reawaken your creativity. Creativity is the absolute essence of who we are as human beings. It's our most basic and fundamental nature, and connecting with and expressing our creativity has a profoundly positive effect on our physical, mental, emotional, and spiritual well-being. If you already know what hobbies and creative pursuits make you feel good, make more time for them in your life. If you've lost touch with your creativity, think back to your childhood. We were all in touch with that part of ourselves when we were young. What did you love to do? What gave you pleasure? Did you enjoy drawing, playing music, writing stories, or being in the garden? If you struggle to come up with ideas, try something new. Spending even short periods of time on your hobbies on a regular basis is the highest quality "me time" you can get, and it does wonders for your self-esteem, happiness, and health.

Acknowledge Your Contribution to the World Around You

Boosting your self-worth can also involve doing "good" things and remembering that you did them. Begin to recognize the myriad skills, talents, and unique gifts that you possess and that you share with those around you. Think about the things you're good at. Reflect on what you do for others on a daily basis. Notice when people compliment you on something. In fact, buy a little notebook and write these compliments down. In this way, you'll be able to acknowledge and appreciate the qualities that others see in you, which otherwise may have just passed you by. This is an effective technique for boosting self-esteem, and your notebook will soon become a permanent source of feel-good energy whenever you feel less than positive about yourself. Look back at your life and remember all your accomplishments. Think about the things you're proud of. If your mind refuses to come up with things, then know that you're not looking hard enough. There is something of worth in every person's life.

Invest in Yourself

Finally, invest in yourself. A key measure of a person's sense of self-worth is the time, energy and resources he or she is willing to expend on himself or herself. Allocate thirty minutes a day to any activity that improves your awareness, develops your talents and potential, enhances the quality of your life, or contributes to the realization of your dreams and aspirations. You can do this through reading books, listening to audio, watching online videos, or attending workshops and courses.

As you begin to develop a healthier attitude towards yourself, you will notice a greater sense of self-respect and self-confidence starting to emerge. You'll find that this makes it easier for you to define and maintain your personal boundaries with others, and that it will make you more willing to speak your truth, because you know that your needs are just as important as the next person's.

Self-Reflection Exercise 6: Learning to Identify and Question Your Unhealthy Beliefs

The first step in moving from passive behaviour to assertive behaviour is to identify and question your unhealthy beliefs, with a view to loosening their hold on you. Then, crucially, you must replace them with healthier beliefs that are in alignment with being assertive. Your beliefs drive your thoughts and your behaviour. Therefore, whenever you want to change how you habitually behave, you must replace an existing belief with a new, more self-serving one. This involves challenging the original unhealthy belief that prevents you from asserting yourself. We have started this process in this chapter.

Now it's time for you to do some work on your own fears and beliefs.

1. Refer back to your responses to self-reflection exercise 5 in chapter 5 and list each of the unhealthy beliefs and fears you identified.
2. Take each unhealthy belief and fear in turn, and ask yourself if it is helpful, valid, and logical. You can do this by writing down your responses to the following questions:
   a. Is the belief or fear going to help you move to a place of assertiveness?
   b. Is the belief or fear in line with reality?
   c. Does the belief or fear make sense?
3. Think about each belief and fear in light of the information included in this chapter and see if you can begin the process of mentally disputing each one and considering whether there is a different viewpoint that might be more helpful—one that serves you better. If you come across any fears and beliefs that feel too overwhelming at this stage, it may help you to remind yourself of the consequences of not moving to a more assertive position in your life. Note all your thoughts and feelings in a journal or notebook.

Thus far, we've focused on the mental skill of disputing. Mentally confronting and disputing unhealthy fears and beliefs is a good place to start because you can begin the process of proving to yourself that those beliefs are untrue, illogical, and unhelpful. However, disputing does not in itself necessarily lead to a shift in emotions. We all know how powerful our feelings can be when it comes to influencing our behaviour. For our behaviour to shift, we must first shift our feelings.

I like to view the mind as a four-door hatchback car and our emotions as a twelve-wheeler lorry. It's much easier for the lorry (our feelings) to push the car (our thoughts) than it is for the car to push the lorry. That's why, when you're trying to change any form of behaviour, you must pay particular attention to the negative feelings that come up, because they have the potential to not only hinder you but also completely halt your journey to assertiveness. In the next chapter, as well as learning how to use your feelings to pinpoint unhealthy beliefs, you'll also learn how to challenge them head-on so you can create lasting change.

7

Chapter

A Road Map for Creating Change in Your Life

So how do you begin to put the ideas we've covered so far into practice and move towards greater assertiveness? In this chapter, I'm going to present a specific model that you can apply in any situation in which you wish to be more assertive.

Rational Emotive Behaviour Therapy

Rational emotive behaviour therapy (REBT) uses an ABC theory of personality to work through a person's emotional and behavioural problems. This ABC framework forms the basis of a process that will enable you to quickly and easily identify the specific beliefs that drive your desire to be quiet and compliant, and to then dispute those beliefs, thus assisting you to change your behaviour.

One of the key tenets of REBT is that events in and of themselves do not have the power to make you feel or behave in a certain way;

your interpretation of the events is the critical aspect. It doesn't matter what happens to you; it's how you understand and make sense of what's happened that's important. Your *interpretation* determines how you *feel* and consequently *behave*.

In the ABC model, A represents the activating event, B represents the underlying beliefs, and C represents the emotional and behavioural consequences. In line with its core tenet, REBT suggests that A (the activating event) does not cause C (the emotional and behavioural consequences), but instead that B (beliefs about A) largely causes C. When something happens that upsets us, we tend to automatically presume it is the event that's had that effect on us, when in fact, in most instances, that is not true. It's the meaning we give to what's happened or to what someone has said that causes the upset.

Zara's experience illustrates this point well. Zara gets angry and upset (C) whenever her husband comes home late from work (A). But it's not the fact that her husband comes home late that causes Zara's emotional response; it's what *she reads into it* (B) that is the real issue.

Similarly, with Jay it's not the fact that his colleagues have all been awarded a pay rise when he hasn't (A) that's the real problem; rather, his interpretation of the situation (B) is what causes him to feel resentful (C).

If, as the REBT model suggests, you contribute to your own psychological problems as well as to the consequent symptoms in the way you interpret events and situations, then it follows that reassessing and reorganizing your beliefs about the situation will enable you to alter your emotional and behavioural responses. The event (A) can remain the same. But if your beliefs about A (i.e., B), change, your emotional and behavioural responses can also change (C).

In Zara's case, she interprets her husband's absence from home (A) as a lack of love and care for herself and their son (B). This is the belief that she has assigned to the situation. This belief evokes a negative emotional response in her, and consequently, she acts in a passive-aggressive manner towards her husband (C).

Jay interprets the situation with his work colleagues (A) as a personal snub (B). He believes his manager is discriminating against him (B), and this conclusion causes him to feel angry towards both his manager and his peers (C).

Since your beliefs determine your emotional and behavioural responses, by questioning and challenging—or "disputing"—your interpretation of situations and events (B), you have the potential to change the way you feel and behave.

Challenging your beliefs, if done persistently, enables you to adopt a different perspective and, in time, to replace the previously unhealthy beliefs with new, healthier, more rational ones. When this whole process is completed successfully, these new thoughts will automatically result in a new set of feelings, which in turn engender a new set of behaviours.

You can apply this model of change to any situation in which you find yourself behaving in a passive way. When you're first learning to use this model, it actually helps to think about it as CAB. The first thing that you usually notice is C, your emotional or behavioural response. This may be a feeling that something isn't quite right, a strong negative reaction to someone or something, or your habitual passive behaviour. Noticing C will help you to identify A, the activating event, which in turn will lead you to reflect on B, your beliefs. It's only then that you will be able to move on to disputing these beliefs so you can arrive at a new, more rational understanding of the situation. This new understanding will result in new feelings that will facilitate new behaviours, which in our case is a more assertive response.

Case Study: Sharon

The best way to understand how this process works in practice is through a case study. Let's start with Sharon. Sharon habitually says yes to requests from work colleagues and friends when, more often than not, she wants to say no. On this occasion, Natasha has asked Sharon if she is available to babysit her three-year-old daughter next Saturday while she attends a training event. Natasha is a long-standing friend and work colleague of Sharon's. Natasha says that this training event takes place in London only once a year and that she's been saving for several months to buy a ticket; if she can't find a babysitter, she won't be able to attend. When she asks Sharon to babysit, Sharon feels put on the spot and believes she has little choice but to agree. As we know, this is Sharon's habitual passive stance.

Let's work through the REBT model and see how Sharon could apply it in this situation so as to move towards responding assertively.

Step 1: Notice the Emotional and Behavioural Consequences (C)

The first thing Sharon notices when she looks back on the incident is that she felt bad when she automatically said yes to Natasha's request. The bad feeling is the emotional consequence (C) of the situation. She wanted to say no because Saturday is her only day off that week and she had planned to spend the time shopping. The fear of saying no and the accompanying guilt compelled Sharon to say yes, even though it wasn't congruent with her truth. Saying yes is the behavioural consequence (C).

Step 2: Identify the Activating Event (A)

Sharon's bad feeling and subsequent passive behaviour arose directly out of the conversation with Natasha, in which Natasha asked her for a favour—a request that Sharon felt she could not refuse. Sharon's activating event, therefore, is saying no to Natasha.

Step 3: Identify the Underlying Unhealthy Belief that Fuelled the Passivity (B)

To identify the underlying beliefs that she holds, it's helpful for Sharon to question what would happen if she were to say no. This course of enquiry unearths the following fears and beliefs: "Natasha will get upset with me. She'll be really disappointed. She's spent a whole year waiting for this event to come to London, and now she won't be able to go. She'll blame me for that, and it'll all be my fault. She won't want to be my friend after that. I hate hurting people's feelings or upsetting them. It makes me feel so awful. I can't deal with that. I'll feel so guilty if I don't help her to go."

If you recall, we learnt in chapter 5 that one of Sharon's biggest fears is people disliking her. She can't bear the thought of other people seeing her as being selfish and upsetting and hurting them. She's also afraid to ask for what she wants and needs because in the past these requests were often met with anger and, on occasion, violence. Sharon believes it's more important for Natasha to get what she wants than it is for her to get what she wants.

It's easy to empathize with Sharon and understand why she felt compelled to say yes when we consider the number of fears that are stacked up against her and preventing her from being assertive.

Unhealthy beliefs share four key characteristics: they involve rigid demands, they "awfulize" (i.e., they lead a person to envisage a situation to be as bad as it can possibly be), they exhibit low frustration tolerance (i.e., they represent the inability to tolerate unpleasant feelings and stressful situations), and they are self-depreciating (i.e., they belittle and denigrate the self).

When Sharon thinks about refusing Natasha's request, the following unhealthy beliefs emerge.

- **Rigid demanding beliefs:** *I must not hurt Natasha's feelings.*

    Sharon lives her life according to this rigid rule: she must never, ever hurt anyone's feelings. This has kept her stuck in a passive stance all her life because she believes that if she doesn't comply with other people's requests or demands, she will hurt or upset them.

- **Awfulizing beliefs:** *Natasha will get so upset with me that she won't want to be my friend. Everything's my fault. It's terrible if I offend or upset Natasha.*

    Sharon tends to overdramatise and overestimate the potential seriousness or negative consequences of her actions. She assumes the absolute worst-case scenario and imagines that the outcome of the situation is going to be as bad as it possibly can be. Sharon's beliefs cause her to put too much focus and value on how awful the potential consequences of asserting herself could be. When she thinks about saying no to Natasha, she catastrophizes and, because she believes there's nothing worse than letting Natasha down, stays stuck in her passive behaviour.

- **Low frustration tolerance beliefs:** *I can't bear it if Natasha feels hurt. I can't bear to let her down.*

    Sharon falsely believes that she lacks the internal resources to cope with the fallout if she doesn't do as Natasha wants. Low frustration tolerance beliefs lead Sharon to assume that she won't be able to endure or withstand the discomfort she will feel if she says no. Consequently, she's convinced herself that saying yes is her only option.

- **Self-depreciating beliefs:** *If I hurt or upset Natasha, it means I'm a bad person.*

Passive behaviour relies on devaluing the self and elevating others. In this case, Sharon is clearly not valuing herself and her needs, but rather making Natasha and Natasha's needs a priority. Sharon further negates her own needs by assigning a value judgement to her actions. She believes that if she doesn't agree to the request, then she is the one who's at fault; she's the one who's being unreasonable; she's the bad person. This belief, coupled with the rigid demanding belief that she must never hurt anyone's feelings, keeps Sharon in a place of passivity where she is forever people-pleasing.

Based on all the above, Sharon's ABC assessment looks like this:

- **A (activating event)**: saying no to Natasha's babysitting request and upsetting her
- **B (beliefs)**: "I must not hurt Natasha's feelings. It's terrible if I offend or upset Natasha. I can't bear to hurt Natasha. If I hurt or upset Natasha, it means I'm a bad person."
- **C (emotional consequence)**: fear and anxiety
- **Behavioural consequence**: agreeing to the request

Step 4: Question the Unhealthy Belief(s)

The next step in the process is for Sharon to question her beliefs. If she discovers that her beliefs do not serve her, she'll have to replace them with more beneficial ones.

The goal when questioning beliefs is threefold: first, you have to recognize that the unhealthy beliefs are indeed unhealthy and do not serve you, then you have to replace the unhealthy beliefs with healthier ones, and, thirdly, you have to convince yourself through forceful reasoning that these alternative beliefs are indeed healthy and will serve you better in the long term.

If Sharon works her way through this whole process, she will be more likely to change her behaviour. It's relatively easy to question and dismantle unhealthy beliefs, but once that task is done, it's essential that those unhealthy beliefs are replaced with healthier ones—ones that you wholeheartedly accept because you *know* they're in *your* best interests.

There are three questions Sharon needs to ask herself when she evaluates each of her beliefs:

1. Is this belief going to help me?
2. Is this belief in line with reality?
3. Does this belief make sense?

Let's examine Sharon's beliefs in the light of these questions.

I must not hurt Natasha's feelings

This belief is clearly not going to help Sharon take a more assertive stance in response to Natasha's request. In fact, it has completely the opposite effect: it locks Sharon firmly into her habitual passive mode.

This belief does not make sense; nor is it in line with reality. The assertion *I must not hurt Natasha's feelings* implies that Sharon is somehow responsible for Natasha's inner world and her responses. This is simply not true. If you recollect our earlier discussion on the principle of emotional responsibility, the responsibility for Natasha's emotional response lies squarely with Natasha, not with Sharon. It's absurd to think that Sharon is so powerful that she can control Natasha's emotional reaction. Furthermore, it's unrealistic to think that a person can go through his or her whole life without ever upsetting another person. A healthy, balanced attitude towards life includes self-care and self-respect. To honour our own thoughts, feelings, and preferences, we must occasionally go against other people's wishes and desires. And if at times other people choose to feel upset by this, it's unavoidable.

It's terrible if I offend or upset Natasha

Is this belief going to help Sharon to be more assertive with Natasha? Clearly not. On the contrary, it ensures that Sharon goes out of her way to let Natasha have what she wants.

Is this belief in line with reality? No. Sharon has made a huge presumption about Natasha's reaction. How does Sharon know for sure that Natasha will be offended or upset? She can't know this with 100 per cent certainty. There's a chance that Natasha may not be upset at all if she understands that Sharon has made other plans. She may acknowledge that she should have given her more notice and not just presumed she was going to agree.

Does this belief make sense? No. Why is it so terrible to offend or upset Natasha? None of us like to be on the receiving end of a negative response from others, but it's not the end of the world, and Natasha's response is her own responsibility, not Sharon's.

I can't bear it if Natasha feels upset

Is this belief going to help Sharon to be more assertive with Natasha? Definitely not.

Is this belief in line with reality? No. If Natasha responds negatively, then Sharon may find herself experiencing some uncomfortable feelings, but is that going to cause her so much distress that "she can't bear it"? Will these uncomfortable feelings have the power to debilitate Sharon to such a degree that she's unable to function in life? I'm guessing not.

Does this belief make sense? No. It overdramatises the situation and underestimates Sharon's ability to cope with some discomfort.

We human beings are incredibly resilient. With a few exceptions (which fall into the realms of severe trauma and mental illness), we all have the innate ability to process and eventually manage our emotional and mental pain without it doing us serious long-term harm. People endure horrendous abuse and can still function. Even in the worst-case scenario, in which Natasha verbally lashes out at Sharon, there's no threat to Sharon's life or safety. She may feel overwhelmed, hurt, and upset, but she will be able to cope. In analysing this belief, Sharon needs to ask herself what it means to not cope with the situation and whether she has made an accurate assessment of her resilience and capacity to withstand negative feelings.

If I hurt or upset Natasha, it means I'm a bad person.

Is this belief going to help Sharon to be more assertive with Natasha? No.

Is this belief in line with reality? No. There is absolutely no link between Natasha being hurt and upset and Sharon being a bad person unless Sharon herself chooses to apply that judgement to herself.

And does it make sense? No. If Sharon had deliberately and maliciously set out to hurt Natasha, then it could be a legitimate belief. But in this case, Sharon's sole intention is not to hurt Natasha but to simply honour her own needs and preferences in the situation.

Step 5: Replace the Unhealthy Beliefs with Healthier Beliefs

Having disputed some of the unhealthy beliefs that Sharon is holding on to, it's now important that she replaces them with a new set of healthier and more rational beliefs.

Healthy beliefs have the following characteristics: they encourage flexible preferences, they foster a rational and realistic viewpoint, they exhibit a high frustration tolerance, and they focus on self-acceptance and self-respect.

Sharon must replace her rigid belief *I must not hurt Natasha's feelings* with a more flexible belief, such as *I certainly don't wish to hurt Natasha's feelings, nor is it my intention to hurt her, but I accept that I can't take responsibility for her reactions. I also accept that I may not be able to go through my whole life without ever upsetting anyone.*

Her awfulizing belief *It's so terrible if I offend or upset Natasha* needs to be replaced with a more balanced belief—for example: *I don't know how Natasha's going to respond when I tell her I'm not available to babysit. She may be upset about the situation, but it won't be the end of the world if Natasha gets upset on this occasion.*

Her low-frustration-tolerance belief *I can't bear it if Natasha feels hurt* needs to be replaced with *I don't want Natasha to be hurt and upset with me, but if she is, I can handle it. It may feel uncomfortable in the moment, but it won't kill me.*

And her self-depreciating belief *If I hurt or upset Natasha, it means I'm a bad person* needs to be replaced with *I'm sorry if Natasha is hurt or upset, because that was never my intention. Like her, I'm a valuable human being, and my needs are of equal importance.*

Sharon's Unhealthy Beliefs	Sharon's New Healthy Beliefs
I must not hurt Natasha's feelings.	*I certainly don't wish to hurt Natasha's feelings, nor is it my intention to hurt her, but I accept that I can't take responsibility for her reactions. I also accept that I may not be able to go through my whole life without ever upsetting anyone.*

It's so terrible if I offend or upset Natasha.	I don't know how Natasha's going to respond when I tell her I'm not available to babysit. She may be upset about the situation, but it won't be the end of the world if Natasha gets upset on this occasion.
I can't bear it if Natasha feels hurt.	I don't want Natasha to be hurt and upset with me, but if she is, I can handle it. It may feel uncomfortable in the moment, but it won't kill me.
If I hurt or upset Natasha, it means I'm a bad person.	I'm sorry if Natasha is hurt or upset, because that was never my intention. Like her, I'm a valuable human being, and my needs are of equal importance.

As you read the two sets of statements side by side, notice how you feel. You should find that the healthy beliefs induce more positive feelings in you than the unhealthy beliefs. Because our feelings play a crucial role in determining our behaviour, adopting new empowered beliefs will make any attempts at assertion much easier.

Case Study: Jay

Let's run through the model again, this time with Jay. As we've already seen, Jay struggles to speak his truth at work. Financially, he's just about making ends meet since he moved into his own studio apartment. Jay wants to ask for a pay rise, but his passive behaviour is preventing him from approaching his manager. The time has come for the annual pay award once again, so this is the perfect time for him to review how he's going to approach the conversation with his boss.

Ever since he started at the company, Jay has had the same experience at the annual appraisal meeting. Each time, he's walked into his manager's office, sat down, and quietly agreed with everything his manager has said about his performance, his targets for the following year, and his salary. Each year, his manager has told him that he's doing a good job and that he'd like him to continue working in the same way. He's never mentioned increasing Jay's pay. This year Jay would like to approach the meeting differently. He would like to be assertive and ask why, if he's been doing a good job and meeting all his targets, he's not eligible for a pay increase.

Step 1: Notice the Emotional and Behavioural Consequences (C)

When Jay thinks about being in the annual review meeting, he notices a tense feeling throughout his body. He's also aware that whenever he thinks about asking his manager for a pay review, his chest tightens, his throat feels constricted, and there is some mild discomfort in his abdomen.

Step 2: Identify the Activating Event (A)

The mere thought of speaking up and asking his manager to review his pay triggers these bodily sensations. To keep these uncomfortable feelings at bay, at previous meetings Jay has chosen to remain silent and agree with what his manager says, rather than asking for what he wants. The meeting is clearly his activating event.

Steps 3 and 4: Identify and Question the Underlying Unhealthy Beliefs that Are Fuelling the Passivity (B)

To identify his underlying beliefs, it's helpful for Jay to question what would happen if he were to speak up and ask his manager for a pay review. This course of enquiry unearths the following fears and beliefs:

> If I ask him for a pay rise, he's probably going to say no. I know he keeps saying that I'm doing a good job, but I'm not sure. He might start going over my work. He might say I'm not performing that brilliantly. I mean, why hasn't he given me a pay rise of his own accord? Isn't it his job to do that? He's probably just saying I'm doing a good job so that we stay on good terms. Maybe other people are doing a better job than me. Maybe I'm hanging on by the skin of my teeth. Who knows?
>
> What if I make a fuss and he reacts badly? I can't risk losing my job. I have all these expenses. If I lose my job, I'll end up losing my apartment, and there's no way I'm going back home. I'll be homeless! It was hard enough to find this job. How the hell am I going to get another one? And if I ask for a pay rise and he refuses, he's going to think I'm a real loser. He might start talking about me in front of the other team members and making fun of me. I know they don't like me. They're all going to have a good laugh. I can't deal with that. I can't bear to look stupid in front of him ... or them.

It's easy to see how Jay's beliefs, fears, and assessment of the situation cause him to feel anxious about asking for a pay review. In chapter 5, we discovered that Jay has little self-confidence; he fears rejection and is petrified of losing his job. The disagreement with his father has forced him to be independent, and his pride will not allow him to go back home if he loses his apartment.

Jay's internal narrative has uncovered a raft of awfulizing beliefs and fears. He starts by assuming the worst: his boss is going to reject his request for a pay increase. He then proceeds to catastrophise all the way to becoming homeless! Let's work through Jay's beliefs with a view to challenging them and changing them into healthier ones.

Jay's reluctance to speak up in the meeting is rooted in the rigid belief *I must not draw attention to myself.* Underneath this belief is the self-depreciating belief that he lacks ability and talent—ability and talent that he automatically assumes all his colleagues possess. Jay's reluctance to ask for a pay review has its roots in this lack of self-confidence. Over time, this has caused Jay to avoid drawing attention to himself; he believes it's safer to stay quietly in the background. Jay firmly believes that if anyone gets too close, he or she will discover just how useless he is, and he strongly fears the consequences of this. Are these beliefs going to help him become more assertive and ask for a pay review? Are these beliefs in line with reality? And do they make sense? The answer to all these questions is no.

If you look at the hard facts, Jay has managed to hold down his current job for six years. He is seriously underestimating his employer's competence, because if he's so incompetent, would he not have been dismissed already? He's had an appraisal every year. He also meets with his manager every quarter to review his targets. If he's been as ineffectual and inefficient as he fears, then undoubtedly his manager would have brought this to his attention at some point over the years. On the contrary, his manager has consistently said that he's doing a good job. But Jay's lack of belief in himself means that his mind doesn't register this positive feedback. The facts indicate that Jay is doing his job just fine. He's not an incompetent worker. So the issue here is not his ability but his belief in his ability. It's his lack of self-confidence that is letting him down, not his ability to do the job.

The beliefs we hold colour everything in our lives. They're like coloured glasses that we permanently wear, and they distort everything we see. Jay's lack of self-confidence makes it difficult for him to hear and trust what his manager is really saying to him. Instead he simply edits out the positive feedback from his mind and clings to the belief that he's not good at his job.

Returning to Jay's inner dialogue, he goes on to reinforce his self-depreciating and rigid beliefs by questioning why his manager hasn't offered him a pay review of his own accord. That Jay is a mediocre worker could be one explanation, but there could be many others. Jay works for a small private company whose key objective is financial profit. There may be an unwritten assumption that if you don't ask for a pay review, you won't get one. His manager may be interpreting Jay's silence on the matter as a sign that Jay is happy with the pay he's getting. Perhaps Jay's colleagues have been assertive enough to ask, and that's why they've negotiated promotions and pay rises.

Jay's lack of confidence must be evident to his manager. It's likely that he's shown a reluctance to step forward and take on more responsibility within the team. It's possible his manager perceives Jay's desire to remain in the background as a lack of ambition. His manager may not have suggested a pay review because Jay's demeanour and behaviour have not warranted one. If Jay wants a salary increase, then he's going to have to earn it by showing his manager that he's done something over and above his current duties or that he's willing to take on new areas of work and responsibility. Jay has wrongly assumed that his manager's unwillingness to offer him a pay rise must mean that he's not good at his job.

Jay's internal narrative highlights a string of negative assumptions. But how true are they? He immediately concludes that his manager will refuse his request. Yet he can't know this for sure. He concludes that he's going to lose his job. Again, he can't know this for sure. He's been a member of the accounts department for six years. As such, he must add some value to the company and perform a vital role; otherwise, he would have been dismissed a long time ago. Jay has also gone as far as visualizing himself losing his apartment and becoming homeless, so he has a tendency to awfulize, too.

If he were to lose his job, is it rational to believe that he would never find another one? After all, he has experience and expertise in what he does. The worst-case scenario, if he did lose his job, would be that he would be unemployed for a time or that he would need to take on some temporary work for a while before he found a permanent role. Jay has seriously overdramatised the situation. It's highly unlikely that he would get into such financial difficulty that he would lose his home. What these fears really suggest is that Jay can't bear the thought of the stress he might incur if he risked asking for what he wants. He has a low frustration tolerance. He's also convinced himself that his manager is going to tell everyone he works with about his personal affairs and that he will become the butt of office gossip, telling himself that he "can't bear to look stupid in front of him … or them."

Taking all the above into account, Jay's ABC assessment looks like this:

- **A (activating event)**: asking his manager for a pay review
- **B (beliefs)**: *I must not draw attention to myself. My manager is going to refuse. My manager will realize I'm not good at my job. I'll lose my job. I won't be able to find another job. I'll lose my flat. I'll be the butt of office gossip. I can't bear my manager and colleagues talking about me.*
- **C (emotional consequence)**: fear and anxiety
- **Behavioural consequence**: not asking his manager for a pay review

Step 5: Replace the Unhealthy Beliefs with Healthier Beliefs

We've started the process of disrupting some of the unhealthy beliefs that Jay is holding on to. The next step is to replace these unhealthy beliefs with a new set of healthy and more rational beliefs—ones that allow flexible preferences, are non-awfulizing, exhibit a high frustration tolerance, and focus on self-acceptance and self-respect. Here's a summary of Jay's new beliefs.

Jay's Unhealthy Beliefs	Jay's New Healthy Beliefs
I must not draw attention to myself.	*I work in a firm as part of a team, and it's my manager's job to pay attention to what I'm doing. It's unrealistic to think I can go through life hiding all the time. It may feel uncomfortable, but I can tolerate the attention if I have to. I have nothing to hide.*
My manager is going to refuse.	*I don't know for sure that my manager is going to refuse. I'm not able to read his mind or accurately predict what he's thinking or going to do. I have to focus on the aspect of this situation that is in my control and not waste my time and energy pre-empting and stressing about things I have no control over.*
My manager will realize I'm not good at my job.	*If my manager thinks I'm not good at my job, then it's his responsibility to tell me. I've held down this job for six years, and in all that time he's never raised a concern. So there's little evidence that I'm not doing my job well.*
I'll lose my job.	*There's nothing to suggest that I'm going to lose my job. I've been at this job for six years. My manager has never had a problem with me, so it's unrealistic to believe I'd be sacked without warning. If there are problems, then I can work with my manager to sort them out. And at the end of the day, even if I did lose my job, my life wouldn't be over. It wouldn't be the end of the world. I'd cope. I'd have my notice period to work through, and I'd look for another job. I have six years of experience.*

I'll lose my apartment.	I won't lose my apartment. It's highly unlikely I'd be sacked from my job, but even if that did happen and I couldn't keep up my mortgage payments, I'd renegotiate my payment plan with the bank. I'd find temporary work until I could get a permanent role. Evictions don't happen overnight. I'd have plenty of time to secure other work if I needed to.
I'll become the butt of office gossip, and I can't bear it.	I have no control over what other people do or say. Neither do I have control over what other people think about me. I'd feel hurt if I knew people were gossiping about me, and it would make me feel upset, but I'd survive. In any case, it's unlikely my manager would share confidential information about me with other people. But if it happens, I can tolerate it. It wouldn't be the end of the world.

Again, notice how you feel when you read over Jay's new healthy beliefs. You'll find that they induce more positive feelings than the unhealthy ones. For this reason, Jay will find it much easier to practise being assertive if he adopts more empowered beliefs.

Self-Reflection Exercise 7: Using What You've Learnt to Tackle a Real-Life Situation

It's now time for you to pick a situation from your own life, practise applying the CAB model to it, and then work at identifying, disputing, and replacing any unhealthy beliefs you discover. Think back to a situation in the past where you wish you'd responded more assertively. Then analyse the situation by working through the following ten steps. It's helpful to write down your thoughts as you go through the exercise.

1. Notice how you felt and what you did. This is the emotional and behavioural consequence (C).
2. Identify the activating event (A). What happened to make you feel and act that way?
3. To detect your underlying beliefs (B), use the journaling exercise where you imagine what would have happened if you'd spoken your truth in this situation.
4. Identify any beliefs that involve rigid demands.
5. Identify any beliefs that awfulize the situation and predict dire outcomes.
6. Identify any beliefs that exhibit a low frustration tolerance.
7. Identify any beliefs that are self-depreciating, where you dismiss or marginalize your own needs and preferences by prioritizing the needs and wishes of others.
8. Taking one unhealthy belief at a time, ask yourself the following questions:
    a. Is this belief going to help me?
    b. Is this belief in line with reality?
    c. Does this belief make sense?
9. Replace any unhealthy beliefs with healthier and more rational beliefs that
    a. allow flexible preferences,
    b. foster a rational and realistic viewpoint,
    c. exhibit a high frustration tolerance, and
    d. focus on self-acceptance and self-respect.
10. Notice how these new beliefs make you feel. You should find that your emotional state shifts to being lighter and more positive when you think about speaking your truth now.

This exercise can be challenging at first, but if you follow the steps diligently and persevere, you will have started the process of disputing your old beliefs and loosening their hold over you.

In this chapter, we've worked at intellectually identifying, disputing, and reframing the beliefs that have prevented you from being more assertive. Now, this may all sound simple in theory, but we all know that changing long-standing beliefs can be very difficult. After all, you've probably been carrying these fears and beliefs around with you for a long time, and they will have shaped your personality and your view of the world. In the next chapter, we're going to explore the ways in which you can deepen your conviction in the new healthier beliefs you'd like to adopt, while at the same time loosening the hold that any unhealthy beliefs have on you.

8
Chapter

How to Internalize Your New-Found Beliefs

It's one thing to accept your new healthy beliefs at an intellectual level, but if they're to become ingrained in you, become part of who you are, you also need to accept them at a deeper emotional level. This takes deliberate *intention*, *focus*, and *commitment*.

It can take a long time to fully integrate this new way of thinking, feeling, and behaving. It would be wrong to suggest that simply disputing and intellectually disrupting disempowering beliefs is going to be enough to change the way you think, act, and feel in any given situation—especially if you've been thinking, acting, and feeling the same way for most of your life. There are, however, two powerful techniques that you can use to imprint your new-found beliefs on your psyche and thus grow to be more assertive.

Our brains have an amazing ability to grow and change throughout our lifetimes. This ability to form new neural connections and eliminate old ones is known as neuroplasticity. Simply put, neural connections allow nerve cells in the brain to connect with and send information to each other. In previous generations, people believed that the neural connections in the brain became fixed by a certain age. We now know this to be untrue.[8] For example, when the brain forms memories or learns new tasks, it encodes the new information by creating new neural pathways. In this way, the brain continues to develop and rewire itself throughout a person's lifetime. We also now know that experience and repetition can change the brain's structure and functioning.

An important concept in neuroplasticity is that of synaptic pruning. Throughout a person's life, the brain eliminates neural connections that are no longer used and rewires and strengthens those that are frequently used. Therefore, if you are to learn a more assertive way of thinking, feeling and acting, you will need to work at creating new neural pathways that effectively change your brain and supersede the old wiring that led to your passive behaviour.

Repetition is the key. Every time you do something for the first time, you create a new neural pathway. If you then continue to repeat that thought or emotion, you reinforce the new pathway until eventually it strengthens enough to become your habitual way of being. That's why intentionally creating a thought or repeatedly taking an action increases its power. Over a period of time, that new thought or action becomes an intrinsic part of who you are, and you naturally start to think and behave in a new way. The awkwardness you felt and the effort you had to put in at the beginning gradually diminish.

---

[8] Bennett, E.L., Diamond, M.C., Krech, D., and Rosenzweig, M.R., "Chemical and Anatomical Plasticity of the Brain", *Science*, 146 (1964), 610–19; Livingston, R.B., "Brain mechanisms in conditioning and learning", *Neurosciences Research Program Bulletin*, 4/3 (1966), 349–54; Rakic, P., "Neurogenesis in adult primate neocortex: an evaluation of the evidence", *Nature Reviews Neuroscience*, 3/1 (January 2002), 65–71.

The two techniques that you can use to reinforce your healthier beliefs are affirmations and rational emotive imagery. Both of these techniques help to first build new neural pathways and then reinforce them, so that you think, feel, and act in accordance with your new assertive beliefs.

Affirmations

Affirmations are positive statements about the self that are forcefully repeated on a regular basis; and they are a powerful transformative tool. Any statement said with confidence and repeated continuously has the power to eventually "overwrite" previously held unhealthy beliefs. Seen as the modern-day equivalent of ancient mantras in terms of their catalytic power, affirmations have the capacity to reprogram your mind and positively affect your emotions.

The human brain is a powerful thing. It's the most complex structure known to man. And it has one attribute that you can take advantage of to improve just about any area of your life. That attribute is that your mind does not know the difference between what is real and what is fantasy; it simply believes what it's repeatedly told.

To test this for yourself, take a moment right now to tune into your body. Notice how much energy you feel you have. Give yourself a score from one to ten, where one represents complete exhaustion and ten represents total vitality. Then sit down and repeat the statement "I'm so tired ... my muscles feel so heavy ... I'm totally shattered" thirty times. Really connect with and *feel* each word. When you've finished, check in with your body again and notice how you feel. As before, give yourself a score out of ten. If you've done the exercise properly, your energy levels should be lower than when you began.

Now repeat the exercise using a positive statement. Say, "I'm full of energy ... I feel strong and revitalized," thirty times. Then give your energy level a score from one to ten. This time you should find

The Power of Speaking Your Truth

that your score is higher. Notice how you've been able to influence how you feel simply by using the power of your mind.

Through deliberate focus and intention, you can use the power of your mind to your advantage. If your mind does not know the difference between what is real and what is fantasy, and it simply believes what it is repeatedly told, then short, positive affirming statements said to yourself over and over again will programme the mind to believe and internalize these statements.

As you will have seen from the unhealthy beliefs we uncovered in the case studies in chapter 7, a person who is habituated to behave passively has a negative internal script playing consciously or unconsciously in his or her mind. Affirmations can be used to directly challenge and overwrite these negative beliefs with more positive ones.

This is best illustrated with some examples, so let's consider which affirmations could help Sharon. You may remember that her negative beliefs centre on not wanting to upset other people and hurt their feelings. The following affirmations would help her overturn some of the negative beliefs that keep her fixed in her passive behaviour.

- I am assertive.
- I speak my truth clearly, calmly, and confidently.
- I value my own beliefs and opinions.
- I communicate my needs to others in a calm and confident manner.
- I stand up for myself and have healthy boundaries.
- My needs are just as important as other people's.
- I have the right to stand up for myself.

Jay's negative beliefs relate to his false assumption that he's incompetent at work and his fears about losing his job if he asks for the pay rise he wants. For Jay, the following affirmations would be helpful:

- I am good at my job.
- I am a valued and respected member of the team.
- I treat people with respect, and they respond accordingly.
- I am intelligent and competent.
- I welcome responsibility; I handle it easily and effortlessly.
- I speak up for myself.
- I am confident in asking for what I want.
- I am safe and equipped to handle any challenges that may arise.

How to Use Affirmations

Affirmations are easy to create and use. Refer to the outcomes of self-reflection exercises 5, 6, and 7, and identify the negative beliefs you are holding and wish to overturn. Then create an affirmation that directly opposes each belief. For example, if you've identified a belief that other people's needs are more important than your own needs, then you could start using the affirmation "My needs are just as important as everyone else's."

When creating affirmations, it's important to apply the following rules.

Firstly, ensure the affirmation is in the present tense. This ensures that your subconscious mind goes to work on the affirmation straight away. Though few people would consider writing a positive self-talk statement in the past tense, many make the mistake of projecting what they want into the future. By saying "I will ..." or "I am going to ...", you're placing your desire somewhere out there in the future, just beyond your reach. Remember: the future doesn't exist yet. Change happens only in the present. Affirming in the

The Power of Speaking Your Truth

present tense also makes it easier for you to generate the necessary emotions and visualizations to support your affirmations. There's a world of difference between saying "I will be so happy when …" and saying "I am so happy now that …"

Secondly, ensure that your affirmations use only positive words. Avoid negative words, such as "no", "not", "never", "don't", "won't", and "can't". You must direct your self-talk *towards* what you want, not away from what you don't want. The reason for this is that your words create the mental images that make up the language of your subconscious mind. When you speak about what you don't want, you literally create that image, and this negative image is what the subconscious mind will work on. By focusing your words on what you do want, you direct the subconscious mind to work on the positive results you desire. This is also why you shouldn't use any words or phrases that imply the negative, such as "get rid of", "give up", "lose", "quit", "stop", "refrain", and "avoid", words that imply being without, such as "I want", "I wish" and "I would like", or words that refer to the problem you wish to resolve. You don't want to inadvertently visualize—and thus reinforce—the very issue you're trying to eradicate.

Thirdly, use strong emotive words to create your affirmations. The subconscious mind picks up and gives importance to those thoughts to which we apply the most emotion or feeling. The more energy and passion you put into your affirmations, the more effective they will be. Use words that inspire and empower you. Use your favourite adjectives to give your words more force. Use words like "exuberant", "incredible", "outstanding", "brilliant" and "fantastic". Use adverbs like "lovingly", "passionately", "consistently", "calmly" and "joyfully". The more emotion you invest in your affirmations, the faster they will work.

Once you've come up with your affirmations, you need to state them as often as you can. There are several ways in which you can do this. You can write them down on a piece of card and carry them around with you as a reminder. You can have them ping up on your phone throughout the day so you can read them regularly. You can say the affirmations aloud for five minutes at least three times a day—in the morning, at midday, and in the evening—for a minimum of forty days (which is the time it takes to establish a new habit or mode of behaviour). You can also record yourself saying your affirmations in a calm, confident way and listen to this recording daily as many times as you can.

As you repeat your affirmations, actively visualize yourself having and using the qualities you're speaking of. So if your affirmation is "I am confident", imagine how you would look and act, what you'd say, how you'd dress, etc., when you're being confident; picture it in as much detail as possible. As we learnt earlier, your brain can't tell the difference between reality and imagination; as far as it is concerned, what you imagine to be happening is actually happening. The repetition, combined with the visualization, will reinforce the new beliefs in your subconscious mind, and in time you'll start to notice the difference within yourself. You'll start to embody these new beliefs, and they'll begin to automatically drive your behaviour.

Rational Emotive Imagery

Rational emotive imagery is another highly effective way of retraining the brain and practising a new way of thinking and acting so as to create new feelings and actions in your life.[9] For our purposes, it involves selecting a specific situation in which you struggle to be assertive and actively using your imagination to practise behaving assertively. This is the opposite of the process that most people engage in when they spend time worrying and imagining that events and situations will have awful outcomes; in other words, they literally

---

[9] Ellis, A., and Dryden W., *The Practice of Rational Emotive Behaviour Therapy*, 2nd ed., Free Association Books, London, 1999.

practise, and reinforce, feeling bad! With rational (or positive) emotive imagery, you literally practise, and reinforce, feeling good.

This technique is slightly different to simply visualizing. When you visualize something positive, you create positive images in your mind, which then evoke positive emotions in you. This process is good for displacing negative images and negative emotions. But with rational emotive imagery, you take it one step further. You don't just visualize positive outcomes and experience the consequential positive emotions; you also visualize yourself *practising* a new way of thinking and acting.

Now, we all know that people and events are unpredictable, and that in real life things may not happen the way we would like them to. You can't always control what happens in life and how other people react, but you can control the way *you think* and the way *you act*.

Rational emotive imagery offers a way of overwriting your old self-defeating thinking patterns with a healthier way of thinking— one that serves you better in the long term. It encourages you to focus on your own thoughts and feelings and how you can positively influence them, as opposed to how others should be acting and behaving towards you. This helps you to move away from the idea that happiness is dependent on factors outside of yourself and reinforces the healthier belief that you are responsible for your own happiness. Even if something unpleasant happens to you, you can still take charge of your thoughts and feelings. At worst, you can neutralize any negative feelings, and at best, you can create more positive ones.

Whenever you practise rational emotive imagery, you're retraining your brain. Whenever you rehearse anything in life, you get better and better at it as you learn how to do it. With continued practice, it eventually becomes a habit, and when something is a habit, it becomes effortless.

The other advantage of rational emotive imagery is that you get to practise without any fear of failure. Being assertive can be a daunting prospect for anyone who has lived passively for most of his or her life. Therefore, expecting yourself to practise in real-life situations, with real people, is probably going to be too much to ask initially. However, if you practise acting assertively in your imagination first, there is little to lose, and there are no consequences if at the beginning you get it wrong or can't do it very well. Doubt, fear, confusion, and mistakes are natural consequences of learning something new. Rational emotive imagery allows you to experience all of these emotions, to re-educate your mind, and to rewire your emotional responses without any negative repercussions. In fact, rational emotive imagery removes the barriers to new learning and speeds up the re-education process.

Self-Reflection Exercise 8: Learning to Use Rational Emotive Imagery

The following exercise takes you through what you need to do to practise rational emotive imagery.

1. Select a situation in which you struggle to speak your truth.
2. Work through self-reflection exercise 7 so you can readily identify the new healthy beliefs that you're trying to internalize. Write them down or record yourself saying them aloud.
3. Relax by breathing deeply and slowly for a few minutes to clear your mind and calm yourself down.
4. Start to visualize what happens during the situation you've chosen to work on; in other words, replay it in your mind. Review what is happening outside of you; note where you are, your surroundings, the people around you, what they're doing, and what you're doing. Become aware of how you feel.

5. Now place your attention on the thoughts that you've decided will help you—the new healthy beliefs you'd like to adopt. (It helps to have them written down and placed in front of you or recorded in your own voice onto a device so you can play them back to yourself.) Repeat these thoughts to yourself and begin to connect with the feelings that are associated with them. It can help to say the statements aloud. Since your new healthy beliefs are positive statements, you should be connecting with positive and empowered feelings. Allow yourself to become totally immersed in these positive feelings, and continue to feel them for as long as you can.
6. Imagine behaving in a more assertive way in this situation. Imagine yourself responding calmly and confidently. Visualize this as many times as you can. What do you say? What do you do? What is your body language? Remember that during this exercise you should be concentrating on your own behaviour, not on how the other person is responding.
7. If (or when) you notice yourself slipping into negative thoughts or feelings, immediately take your mind back to your positive, healthy thoughts, reconnect with the good feelings they evoke, and go back to visualizing being assertive again.

If you can't quite focus your mind on this exercise, because you sense you're either not wholeheartedly accepting the new beliefs or getting in touch with the positive feelings, notice what thoughts keep arising. What doubts, reservations, and objections come up for you? It's helpful to write them down. They may be different each time you do the exercise, depending on how you're feeling at the time. All this information is incredibly useful because it helps you to identify what is blocking you from being assertive. Once you've identified each block, you can then actively work on overturning the unhealthy beliefs behind it by using affirmations or visualizations, before returning to the exercise.

If you struggle to summon up the feelings you're looking for—which, for example, could be enthusiasm and confidence—then it can be useful to identify a time in your life when you experienced the emotions that you're trying to connect with now, and to then spend five minutes remembering, visualizing, and hence reinforcing those positive emotions. For example, if you're looking for courage, then ask yourself, *When in my life have I felt courageous?* Identify a time when you were the most courageous. Where were you? What were you doing? Really connect with the feeling of courage. How does it feel to be courageous? Notice where the sensations of courage sit in your body. Perhaps you can give the feeling of courage a colour and imagine this colour saturating the whole of your body. See this colour emanating from you until you're totally immersed in a bubble of pure courage. Tap into the energy of this feeling as much as you can. Spend a few minutes fully embodying the quality of courage, and when you're totally immersed in it, go back to the original visualization exercise and have another go at envisioning being assertive.

By identifying and actively working on each of the blocks that presents itself, you can gradually weaken and dissolve your internal barriers to being assertive.

Overturning unhealthy beliefs requires persistence. Beliefs can be deeply entrenched in our psyches, so you may have to return to the task of reviewing your beliefs time and again and consciously work at overturning the ones that are getting in your way. It can help to write out the scenario you're working on as a narrative in which you have the starring role. This will enable you to become very clear about how you want to think, feel, and act. For example, "When x happens, I think ... then I feel ... and then I say ..." Writing out the visualization means you can reread the prompts and get straight into visualizing. You can continue to re-visualize until you become familiar with and confident in your new way of behaving. Rest assured that every time you visualize thinking, feeling, and acting in a certain way, you're strongly reinforcing this new way of being in your mind and negating your previous unhealthy way of living.

Case Study: Jasmine

Let's work through an example with Jasmine. As you may remember, Jasmine is a thirty-two-year-old mother of two who lives with her extended family. Jasmine wants to tell her mother-in-law that she will be attending a yoga class every Tuesday evening from 7.00 p.m. to 8.00 p.m., and that she will be out of the house between 6.30 p.m. and 8.30 p.m. Jasmine is acutely aware of the fact that this is the family's busy dinner time slot and that she plays an active daily role in cooking and serving dinner and clearing up afterwards. When she thinks about informing her mother-in-law that she won't be available to do this, Jasmine's deepest fears kick in and stop her from saying what she wants to say. You may recall that she fears disapproval, judgement, rejection, and criticism. She's also worried about letting others down and being perceived as selfish. In addition to all this, Jasmine fears her own negative emotional reactions, and this means that she shies away from confrontation.

Having done the earlier exercises to identify and dispute her fears and the beliefs she holds, Jasmine eventually arrives at a new set of healthier beliefs:

- *I'm at home six out of seven evenings a week. I contribute a lot to the family, so it's okay for me to take one evening out for yoga.*
- *My needs are just as important as anyone else's.*
- *If I feel uncomfortable, it's okay; I can handle it.*
- *If people disagree with me, I can cope; it's not the end of the world.*

She writes down these beliefs on a piece of paper which she places on her lap as she does the rational emotive imagery exercise. This way she's very clear about what her new beliefs are. Jasmine picks a time when she knows no one will disturb her. She spends a few moments focusing on her breath and takes several deep, slow breaths to clear and calm her mind.

Jasmine closes her eyes and visualizes herself entering the living room. She sees her mother-in-law sitting on the sofa. Her son is kneeling on the floor to the right of her, playing with his Lego bricks. The television is on; she can hear the muffled voices of the actors in the soap opera her mother-in-law is watching. Her father-in-law is sitting in an armchair, reading the local paper. It's a warm day, and the sun is streaming in through the voile curtains. One of the windows is open, and she can hear cars driving past and a dog barking in the distance. Jasmine visualizes herself entering the room and sitting on the armrest of the sofa, with her body slightly tilted towards her mother-in-law. She checks in with herself and notices that she feels nervous. She notices her breathing is fast and a little shallow, so she spends a few moments quietly focusing on her breath. Deliberately taking several deep, slow breaths helps to calm her down.

Jasmine now begins to focus on her new beliefs. She looks down at the piece of paper on her lap and reads out each one. She places all her attention on *I'm at home six out of seven evenings a week. I contribute a lot to the family, so it's okay for me to take one evening out for my yoga class. My needs are just as important as anyone else's. If I feel uncomfortable, it's okay; I can handle it. If people disagree with me, I can cope; it's not the end of the world. Whatever the outcome, I'll be okay.* She rereads these statements several times and notices the calm, empowered feelings that arise within her. She focuses on the words and allows the associated feelings to intensify.

Next she recalls how confidently she told her husband she was going to start attending the yoga class. She already knows what it

The Power of Speaking Your Truth

feels like to be confident and fearless. She begins to feel the power of that feeling in her abdomen. She starts to feel strong and grounded. Jasmine imagines that this empowering energy is a ball of yellow light and sees it filling her stomach and the area around it. She knows this is where she experiences the physical sensations of anxiety. She focuses on the words "strong", "calm" and "empowered".

When she feels strong and stable, Jasmine visualizes herself turning to face her mother-in-law, looking her in the eye, and clearly and assertively saying, "Mum, I've been told that yoga can help with my anxiety, so I've decided to go to the weekly yoga class at the leisure centre. The class is every Tuesday evening from seven o'clock to eight o'clock. I'll have to leave at six thirty and won't be back until eight thirty. Do you think you can handle dinner on those days?"

Jasmine now turns her attention to her body language. She sees herself with her shoulders relaxed, looking directly at her mother-in-law. In keeping with her personality, she visualizes speaking clearly but in a gentle tone. Jasmine sees herself being calm, relaxed, and controlled. She returns to her breath and ensures that she's still breathing deeply and slowly. She focuses on the colour yellow, which to her signifies inner strength and power.

Five more times, Jasmine visualizes herself entering the living room and speaking to her mother-in-law in the same way. Each time, the exercise becomes easier and more natural. She notices that, initially, her mind had wanted to catastrophise and imagine her mother-in-law reacting negatively. To counteract this, Jasmine reminded herself that the visualization exercise has nothing to do with controlling her mother-in-law's responses; it is solely about practising and becoming comfortable with a new mental and emotional process so she can change her own behaviour. She also reminded herself that she doesn't know for sure what her mother-in-law is going to say, so it's unwise to imagine the response is automatically going to be "No, you can't go."

Jasmine does this visualization exercise several times over three days. By the third day, she notices that she feels considerably less anxious and much more comfortable about having the conversation with her mother-in-law. She now allows herself to reflect on her negotiating position in case her mother-in-law does not respond positively. Jasmine remembers that being assertive is not about always getting her own way; it's about listening to the other person's views and then arriving at a mutually agreeable compromise. Jasmine has known her mother-in-law for almost ten years. She knows that she is not an unreasonable or unkind woman, so there is no rational reason for her to respond negatively. But to prepare for the possibility that she is unhappy with Jasmine's decision, Jasmine visualizes what she would do in that scenario. She imagines being calm and controlled and explaining that her husband has agreed to help with the dinner time chores, and that she needs to attend the class for the sake of her health and well-being.

Rational emotive imagery is a powerful catalyst for inner change. Its purpose is to retrain the brain and convert irrational, unconscious thinking into rational, deliberate thinking. As with anything in life, the more you practise it, the better you'll become at it. Practice really does make perfect. And if you use the technique consistently, you'll start to feel stronger, more confident, and more positive. As you get better at it, your new way of relating to others will come more easily, until eventually it becomes a habit and then a part of who you are.

The trick is to do some concentrated work on this issue for at least one month. It's a good idea to pick one situation in which you notice you behave passively and to focus your practice solely on that scenario until you get the hang of it. (It's best to pick a relatively straightforward situation involving reasonable people so you don't overwhelm yourself.) Do the ABC analysis we covered in chapter 7, and then practise the rational emotive imagery process as often as you can. Continue this practice until you notice a change in the way you feel during the visualization. It does take effort, but if you think about the short- and long-term consequences of not speaking your truth, you'll know that it is well worth making the effort. Once you've mastered the technique, you can then move on to a more challenging situation and apply the process to that until you feel your passive approach to life is beginning to shift.

The vital skills you will develop through this practice are rational thinking and self-determination (i.e., the process by which you control your own life). Not only will you feel better about yourself, but it will also help you to make better decisions and solve problems more effectively. Ultimately, you'll be better able to manage your inner world, to manage your life, and to generate your own happiness, no matter what is going on around you. That is a very empowering place to be.

Chapter 9

Additional Sources of Help on your Assertiveness Journey

We all know that humans are complex beings. The reasons we think, feel, and behave as we do often lie deep within our subconscious, and even our unconscious, minds. In this chapter, we will explore a range of additional supportive tools and approaches that work at a much deeper level than our intellectual minds and our emotions.

One of the reasons you struggle to speak your truth may be because there are blocks lurking deep down, which act as a barrier. So far, we've covered strategies for dealing with the blocks that you're consciously aware of. In this chapter, we will be looking at ways of dealing with issues that are at a hidden, more energetic level. (By "energetic" I mean relating to the flow of energy within your body, mind, emotions, and soul.) This chapter focuses on the parts of yourself that you may not be consciously aware of. But first we need a quick introduction to the human energy field.

Scientists recognize that the entire universe is made up of energy and that all energy is in a constant state of movement, or vibration. Ervin Laszlo writes in *The Intelligence of the Cosmos* that

> A science offering insight into the nature of the world around us needs to offer an account of the origins of that world. The paradigm emerging in science offers a new account of these origins. It is an account of the origins of a world that is basically not material: indeed, matter as such does not exist in this world. The new paradigm takes account of the fact that when we descend to the lowest level accessible to observation and measurement, we do not find bits and pieces of matter: what we find are sets and clusters of vibration. These vibrations constitute the basic reality of the world.[10]

The rate at which this energy vibrates dictates how solidly we perceive it through our senses. For example, if energy is vibrating slowly, then we perceive it as being physically solid and tangible. Take a pebble, for instance. You can see it, you can touch it, and you can feel it. The energy in air, however, vibrates at a higher rate. You can feel a breeze against your skin, so you know it's there, but you can't hold it in your hands or see it with your eyes. It's less tangible than the pebble. Likewise, there are things around us that we know are there even though we can't perceive them with any of our senses. Mobile phone signals are a modern-day example.

The faster energy vibrates, the less tangible it becomes. Our senses can perceive only a limited range of energy vibration. We

---

[10] Laszlo, E., *The Intelligence of the Cosmos*, Inner Traditions, Vermont, 2017.

know, for example, that our ears pick up only a partial range along the full sound spectrum. Some animals can hear sounds that we can't. Similarly, we know that our eyes are sensitive to a very narrow band of frequencies within the enormous range of frequencies that exist on the electromagnetic spectrum. There are several different levels of energy surrounding us, and we perceive only some of them.

The energy field surrounding the human body is understood to be an egg-shaped structure made up of many different layers, each vibrating at a higher frequency than the previous one. You may think that you are one undifferentiated physical being, but you are much more than that. It's rather like a set of Russian nesting dolls; you start with one, but as you unstack them, another one appears, then another one, and then another one, and so on. In a similar way, there are multiple energetic layers surrounding your physical body which are interconnected and interact with one another.

You know you have a physical body. There is no disputing that. This is the densest part of you—the part you are consciously aware of. This is where physical sensations are experienced. At the next level of vibration, there is a web of energy known as the etheric body. It has the same shape as the physical body and penetrates it into the organs, nerves, muscles, bones, etc.

Alternative and complementary therapists commonly acknowledge and work on this energy field. If you've ever had a reflexology or acupuncture treatment, engaged in yoga or any type of martial art, or experienced reiki, you have worked directly with your etheric energy field. This field is composed of energy that has been called different things in different traditions. Scientists refer to it as electromagnetic energy, the Far Eastern traditions refer to it as chi, and the Indian traditions call the energy prana. The etheric energy field consists of numerous energy channels called *nadis*, or meridians, and many alternative and complementary therapies are based on the understanding that blocks in these channels cause ill health, which can manifest as mental unrest, emotional disturbances, or physical disease and illness.

Energy healing works directly with the unseen energetic aspects of a person's being and his or her life. It promotes mental, emotional, physical, and spiritual health by clearing blocks in the energy channels of the body, thereby enhancing the free flow of life force energy. Improving the flow of energy in the energy field supports the self-healing capacity of the body and allows a person to feel happy, healthy, and strong, and to function fully.

So what does all this have to do with assertiveness? Well, ingrained patterns of passive behaviour may have caused, or may be the result of, blockages or issues within your energy field. These blockages may now be inhibiting you and preventing you from changing your behaviour.

When it comes to assertiveness, there are two common energetic issues that need to be explored. The first is a possible blockage in the energy centre associated with speaking, communication, and expression. This is linked to the throat. And the second is the energetic impact of deep unresolved fears, which may be unconsciously affecting you in the present. Because both of these issues exist at an energetic level, the only way to deal with them effectively is at an energetic level.

The good news is that there are a number of holistic therapies and tools you can use to clear energetic blocks and support you on your journey towards greater self-confidence and assertiveness. Most of these are things you can learn to do yourself at little or no cost.

Working to Balance the Throat Chakra

We spoke earlier about the human energy field and the subtle flow of energy through the meridian lines. In several places around the body, there are concentrated spirals of energy. These are known as the chakras. ("Chakra" is a Sanskrit word meaning "wheels of light". Chakras are so called because the energy spins and rotates.) There are many chakras that exist in the various dimensions of your being. Each chakra is important because it regulates a specific part of the brain and endocrine system and supports the health of the emotional body. The image below shows the seven main chakras and the quality associated with each one.

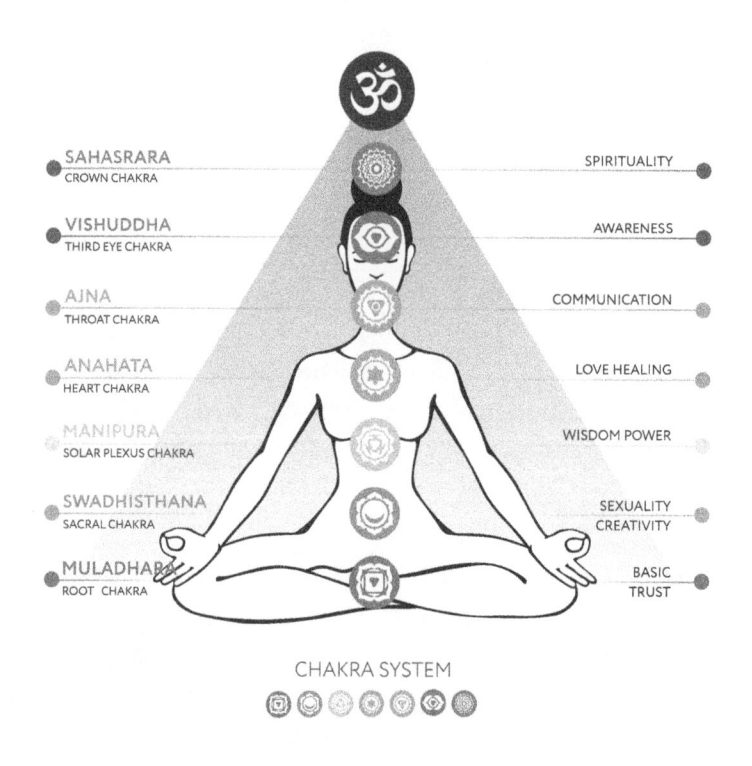

SAHASRARA — CROWN CHAKRA	SPIRITUALITY
VISHUDDHA — THIRD EYE CHAKRA	AWARENESS
AJNA — THROAT CHAKRA	COMMUNICATION
ANAHATA — HEART CHAKRA	LOVE HEALING
MANIPURA — SOLAR PLEXUS CHAKRA	WISDOM POWER
SWADHISTHANA — SACRAL CHAKRA	SEXUALITY CREATIVITY
MULADHARA — ROOT CHAKRA	BASIC TRUST

CHAKRA SYSTEM

The Human Chakra System

When the chakras are open and spinning healthily, you feel happy, healthy, and balanced. Your outlook on life is positive. You are full of vitality. Your blood, your hormones, and your organs all work in perfect harmony, and you feel emotionally balanced. When the chakras are blocked or out of balance, you feel unwell. This can manifest as feeling listless, tired, out of sorts, or depressed. Not only are your physical bodily functions affected in a negative way, allowing disease to manifest, but your thought processes and your mind are also affected. A negative attitude, fear, and doubt can preoccupy a person.

All feelings of unease and ill health can be traced back to the chakra system, and that's why it's been used for millennia to identify the root cause of physical, mental, emotional, and spiritual problems. Working with the chakras targets healing at the deepest level and leads to balance and internal harmony.

The one chakra that is specifically useful to work with when you're learning to speak your truth is your throat chakra. This is blue in colour and, as the name suggests, is situated at the throat. It governs your ability to truly express yourself and to communicate honestly and freely from the heart. If you tend not to speak your truth, there's a high chance that your throat chakra is blocked. This is the result of many years of suppressing the energy of your emotions and being unable to express yourself.

We know that our emotions arise from the core of our being and move through us. Anger is a good example. Cast your mind back to the last time you felt angry. Can you remember the physical sensations running through your body—the tensing of your muscles, the tightness in your stomach, and the uncomfortable pressure rippling up into your throat? There was certainly something erupting from deep within that was seeking acknowledgment and expression.

Emotions always carry deep messages for you if you pay attention and reflect on them. Anger, for instance, is an attack energy. It alerts you to the fact that someone or something has violated your personal boundaries in some way. Its function is to energize you to defend yourself and, if necessary, attack another, with the aim of winning. When anger comes up into the upper torso, it is seeking expression; the energy seeks to move down your arm and out of your fist (impelling you to punch someone) or to come out of your mouth in the form of words to protest or protect yourself. If you've been programmed to stay quiet no matter how you're feeling or what situation you're facing, the energy of anger ascends but then gets stuck in your throat. Your mind literally blocks the energy and stops you from saying anything at all. Over time, this buildup of energy causes a major energetic block.

We can see the problems that a blocked throat chakra can cause in Zara. She rarely speaks her truth. She gets very angry at her husband, but every time her anger tries to surface, she blocks it. Over the years, this constant suppression has caused an accumulation of negative energy in her throat. The negative force field has affected her thyroid gland, which sits directly in front of her throat chakra, and she has developed hypothyroidism, otherwise known as an underactive thyroid gland. As the thyroid gland governs the body's metabolism, this energy block has manifested in her physical body as fatigue, weight gain, hair and skin problems, and a depressed mood. Many people with thyroid conditions have an imbalanced throat chakra. They are not good at speaking their truth.

If you experience persistent and recurring issues in your throat, thyroid and parathyroid glands, neck, vocal cords, other vocal organs, mouth, teeth, gums, jaw, ears, or facial muscles, then you may have a blocked throat chakra. Other symptoms include a fear of speaking; a low, weak voice; difficulties putting feelings into words; shyness; tone deafness; and a poor sense of rhythm. A balanced throat chakra is characterized by a strong, resonant voice; a good sense of timing and rhythm; and clear, open, and honest communication.

A blockage in the throat chakra can lead to considerable discomfort, but fortunately there are many practices you can do that will help to unblock the energy in this part of the body. It's often helpful to start with stretching exercises that focus on moving and loosening tension in the shoulders and neck. Yoga postures that focus on the shoulders and neck area are particularly effective, as are regular neck and shoulder massages. You can also use your voice to regularly draw fresh, healthy energy through your throat chakra. Activities like singing, chanting, humming, and whistling all help this process, and when they are done regularly, they start to dissolve stagnant and blocked energy. Ultimately, the lesson the throat chakra is inviting you to learn is that you are able to comfortably express your innermost truths.

The throat chakra is formed between the ages of seven and twelve years. Any traumatic experiences or emotional difficulties at that stage of your life may have damaged this chakra. If you weren't able to express your feelings because you were too young to understand what was going on or you weren't permitted to communicate your thoughts and feelings because of your family's or your culture's expectations, then your throat chakra will not have developed in a healthy way.

Sharon's childhood experiences have created a block in her throat chakra. You may recall that she grew up in a very dysfunctional and chaotic family. Her father drank heavily, and her mother had mental health problems. She was also removed from her parents' care and sent off to live with her elderly grandmother. Sharon experienced some emotionally difficult situations as a child. And being so young, she lacked the emotional intelligence and capacity to deal with her feelings. So she suppressed them, and they remained unexpressed.

Exploring your past with the help of a therapist can help if you feel that your struggle to be assertive is due to childhood difficulties. Becoming aware of the negative emotions that may be trapped in your body, and then giving yourself time and space to acknowledge and express those emotions, is a powerful way to shift stagnant energy. The talking process naturally and gently allows this energy to flow so that blockages are cleared.

Therapeutic Writing

Another effective and easy way to clear energy blocks in the body is through therapeutic writing. Therapeutic writing is a powerful healing strategy that can significantly enhance your ability to start speaking your truth. In fact, it's a wonderful precursor to speaking your truth because, first of all, it lays down the foundations of your new practice by allowing you to connect with your innermost thoughts and feelings, and secondly, it helps you to express those thoughts and feelings in a safe and controlled way. Therapeutic writing also enhances your creativity, which supports the healthy, free flow of energy through the throat chakra, thereby releasing any energetic blocks.

Anyone can do therapeutic writing; you don't need to be good at writing to try it. You can forget about spelling, grammar, punctuation, and sentence construction. You don't even have to write in sentences. You can just write down words that express how you see things and how you feel. All you need to do is grab a pen and a piece of paper and start writing down anything and everything that comes to mind. What's more, you can do it in the comfort and privacy of your own home.

The health benefits of writing therapy have been well documented.[11] Numerous research findings have shown that writing

---

[11] Baikie, K. A., and Wilhelm, K., "Emotional and physical health benefits of expressive writing", *Advances in Psychiatric Treatment*, 11 (2005), 338–46; Smyth, J. M., Stone, A. A., Hurewitz, A., and Kaell, A., "Effects of writing about stressful experiences on symptom reduction in patients with asthma or rheumatoid arthritis: A randomized trial", *Journal of the American Medical Association*, 281 (1999), 1304–9; Tartakovsky, M., "The power of writing: 3 types of therapeutic writing", Psych Central (2015). Retrieved from https://psychcentral.com/blog/archives/2015/01/19/the-power-of-writing-3-types-of-therapeutic-writing/.

about traumatic, stressful, or emotional events leads to improvements in both physical and psychological health. When people who'd had a therapeutic writing intervention were tracked over subsequent months, they showed a range of improvements, including an improved mood, lower blood pressure, better vital organ functioning, fewer depressive symptoms, better immune system functioning, and fewer traumatic thought intrusions and associated avoidant behaviour. These benefits arise from the fact that therapeutic writing helps you to explore and work through your thoughts and feelings and to unravel and make sense of knotty emotions. It also heightens self-awareness and allows you to develop critical, as well as reflective, awareness.

You can use therapeutic writing to keep a record of your experiences and ideas, and to think things through in a flexible and experimental way. It's also been shown to help people reclaim lost memories and unearth beliefs that were previously unconscious. That's why writing is helpful in exploring the fears that act as internal barriers to assertiveness.

There are several different ways in which you can write therapeutically. Here are three types to experiment with: journaling, composing poetry, and letter writing.

Journaling

Journaling—or free writing—is simply writing about whatever is on your mind or whatever comes up for you in the moment. One way of describing it is as a thought or emotion dump! It literally takes the energy out of your mind and body and transfers it onto paper, giving you instant relief and clarity. You can make it a consistent daily or weekly practice, or you can do it specifically at times when you're struggling with difficult or strong emotions.

Very few people have ever been taught to manage their emotions effectively. Most of us do the thing that's easiest in the moment, which is to push down difficult feelings and then attempt to ignore them. While this can be a good short-term strategy, in the long run it becomes problematic. That's because there comes a point when this energy cannot be suppressed any longer and it begins to bubble up in order to be released, often creating distress and turmoil on its way in the form of physical or mental imbalance.

At such times, when the intensity of your emotions may be threatening to overwhelm you, writing about your feelings can help you to manage the energy more effectively. If you acknowledge what you're feeling; what triggered your emotions; when, where, and how it happened; and who was involved, it allows the energy to flow and be released. You just let it all out. Eventually, if you do this consistently, you will arrive at a place of peace, and an even greater awareness and understanding of what caused the unrest in the first place.

Aside from the fact that it helps you to express your anger, guilt, shame, fear, disgust, grief, and any other difficult feeling, thus reducing the intensity of these emotions in the moment, the other wonderful thing about this sort of free writing is that it is harmless to your relationships, because no one is ever going to read what you've written. In fact, it can even benefit your relationships because it makes it less likely that your feelings will spill out in a damaging way.

If you're processing difficult emotions, once you've "dumped" your thoughts and feelings onto paper, you can symbolically destroy what you've written by shredding or burning the paper in a safe manner, such as in a fireplace. This can be deeply cathartic and will help you to let go of difficult experiences.

As you journey along the road to assertiveness, a useful daily or weekly journaling exercise could be to notice, reflect on, and write about the times when you wanted to speak up but didn't. What were you scared of? What did you really want to say? How did you feel? This activity can be a highly effective way of dealing with any situation in which you notice yourself being passive.

Composing Poetry

Now, I'm not going to profess to be a great writer of poetry, but I have worked with clients who've written some amazingly deep and powerful pieces of verse. Their poetry has succinctly captured and given voice to incredibly painful memories and feelings—feelings they were struggling to articulate through simply talking in our sessions. In all cases, the writing process resulted in deep healing because it allowed buried emotions to gently rise to the surface of the conscious mind, where they were acknowledged, explored, and resolved. Interestingly, like peeling away the layers of an onion, this type of creative writing unearths deeper and deeper layers of buried emotions which seem to automatically present themselves for expression.

If you'd like to ease yourself into writing poetry, then try this exercise from John Fox's book *Poetic Medicine: The Healing Art of Poem-Making*.[12] Pick a memory from your childhood. Maybe start with a happy one, such as a birthday party or a special holiday. Recall all the sensations you experienced at the time: what you saw, smelled, heard, felt, and tasted. Really engross yourself in this memory; allow every aspect of the memory to be absorbed into your body, as though you're reliving the experience right now. Then write down the emotions that came up for you. Staying in touch with your senses, see if you can connect to your inner voice to pen a poem about your experience and how it made you feel. You never know—you may discover a hidden talent! If you do find your creative juices beginning to flow, you could move on to writing about your feelings around not speaking up.

---

[12] Fox, J., *Poetic Medicine: The Healing Art of Poem-Making*, Tarcher Putnam, New York, 1997.

Letter Writing

Therapeutic letter writing is another powerful exercise you can do in connection with anyone with whom you have unfinished business. Persistent, recurring bouts of anger, guilt, regret, and sadness often stem from thoughts such as *If only I'd said this or that, I wouldn't feel so bad* [or *guilty, angry,* or *upset*] *now*. Addressing someone directly by writing a letter to him or her gives you a voice. It allows you to speak your truth, get your point of view across, and gain greater clarity and understanding regarding the situation you're unhappy about. For example, you could write a letter to someone you find it very difficult to stand up to, expressing openly and honestly how you feel.

Ironically, you don't even have to send the letter to feel better. In fact, it's often advisable not to send it unless you know for sure that the contents of the letter are going to be honoured and received graciously. Usually, writing the letter is in itself sufficient to help you process difficult feelings, bring a sense of closure to a fraught relationship, and shift any stagnant energy that may be blocking your throat chakra.

I believe we can all be creative if we give ourselves a chance to try. Often, we don't truly know our thoughts until we try to put them into words. Words act as a medium for expression and a catalyst for clarity—or at least illumination. As a therapist, I see the therapeutic power of verbal communication first-hand. But sometimes, even in the safety of the therapeutic relationship, it can be extremely difficult to put things into words—to express ourselves, our deepest feelings, our thoughts, and our secrets, and to say what we really mean. Sometimes the person that we really want to share our thoughts and feelings with is not available, or we're not able to reveal this part of ourselves to that person for fear of recrimination and negative consequences. This can leave us feeling stuck, isolated, frustrated, and saddened. Therapeutic writing can play a vital role in helping to relieve such feelings and moving you to a state of inner peace and balance.

More Ways to Unblock Your Energy

We're now going to look at several other alternative therapies that can help you to both release energetic blocks in the throat chakra and deal with any unconscious fears or emotions that are keeping you from being assertive.

Emotional Freedom Technique

As we saw in chapter 5, one of the biggest barriers to assertiveness is fear. Fear, in its many guises, literally stops us from speaking our truth. Any form of therapy that helps you to work on and reduce your fear will help you to master being assertive.

Emotional Freedom Technique (EFT) is one such therapy.[13] Popularly known as tapping, it's a relatively new discovery in the field of energy psychology. It provides a quick and simple method for reducing the stress associated with a concern or issue and reprogramming your negative thoughts and beliefs around that concern or issue to more positive ones. Using this technique specifically on the fears you have around being assertive will relieve the intensity of the negative emotions involved, and in time this will free you to say what you need to say when you need to say it. It deals directly with the emotions that keep you stuck in your passive behaviour.

EFT is based on the subtle energy system of acupuncture meridians that was discovered by the Chinese some five thousand years ago. These acupuncture meridians, which run throughout the body, are like internal streams or rivers that are flowing with energy.

---

[13] Ortner, N., *The Tapping Solution*, Hay House UK Ltd, London, 2013.

Just as a river provides life-giving water to the areas that surround it, these channels distribute revitalizing energy to the surrounding areas of the body. When the channels become blocked, they cause problems at every level of your being: physical, mental, emotional, and spiritual.

Gary Craig, the founder of EFT, has said that "The cause of all negative emotions is a disruption in the body's energy system." The acupuncture meridians, which are situated just beneath the surface of the skin, act like energy circuits, conducting currents of energy. If these circuits are disrupted, emotional and physical discomfort results.

In EFT, fingers (as opposed to the needles used by acupuncturists) are used to tap on the end points of the energy meridians. When you do this at the same time as focusing on the specific problem you're trying to resolve, blocks and disruptions are cleared and energy is able to flow freely. The combination of placing your attention on the problem and sending kinetic energy to your energy system facilitates a "straightening out" of the energy system, thus clearing away any disruptions and eliminating the resulting emotional response or its intensity. In this way, emotional harmony is restored.

It's easier to understand how a basic EFT session works by watching one of the many free online videos available. For example, there are some great resources available on the website of The Tapping Solution (www.thetappingsolution.com). The basic technique requires you to focus on the negative emotion that's troubling you—in our case, this is the fear and anxiety around speaking up. While maintaining your mental focus on this issue, you use your fingertips to tap five to seven times on specific points on your body (see the illustration below). Tapping on these meridian points while concentrating on accepting and resolving the negative emotion (through saying certain statements aloud) allows you to access your body's energy field and restore it to a balanced state.

Here's the basic method for an EFT session:

1. Start by identifying the problem and creating a specific phrase that encapsulates how you feel. As an example, we're going to use the phrase "I'm afraid of speaking my truth, because the last time I did, it caused an argument." This may or may not be true for you, but that doesn't matter for now, because we're just using it to illustrate the process. You can replace this statement with one that is more appropriate for you when you're ready to give EFT a go yourself. The phrase you choose should capture the emotional essence of the problem and the reasons this emotion has come up for you, and it can even include any bodily sensations you experience.
2. Once you've connected with the feeling of fear, give it a rating from zero to ten (where zero is no fear at all and ten is extreme fright) to pinpoint how strongly you're feeling the emotion right now. This will help you to track your progress.

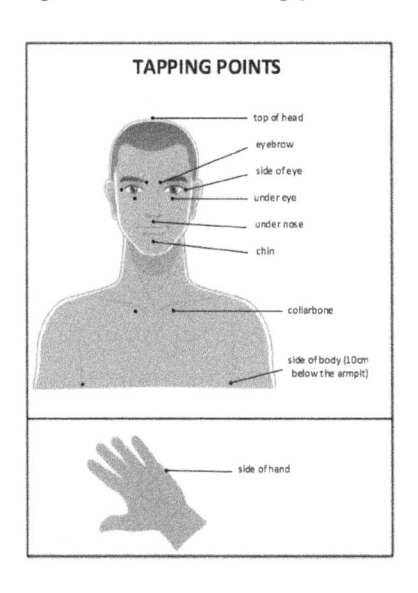

TAPPING POINTS

- top of head
- eyebrow
- side of eye
- under eye
- under nose
- chin
- collarbone
- side of body (10cm below the armpit)
- side of hand

EFT Tapping Points

3. Tap the karate chop point on your hand while repeating the following phrase three times: "Even though I'm afraid of speaking my truth, because the last time I did it caused an argument, I deeply and completely love and accept myself." Place extra emphasis on the second half of the statement as you say it aloud.

   Some people find it difficult to say out loud, or even whisper, that they love and accept themselves, because at some level they feel it's untrue. The thing to remember is that you're reprogramming the mind, and this place of love and acceptance is where you eventually need to move to. If you persevere, it will become easier for you to accept this statement.

4. Starting at the top of the head, work through all the tapping points, repeating the phrase "I'm afraid of speaking my truth, because the last time I did, it caused an argument" three times at each point.
5. When you've finished, take a deep breath and assess how you feel. Has the fear subsided? (At the beginning you may have to do this exercise a few times to notice a shift, so don't give up if at first you don't detect a change.) Persevere and you should find that the fear has subsided a little. Give your current feeling of fear a rating from zero to ten, as before.
6. If you find the fear is still there, you can repeat the whole process again, or you can slightly amend the statement to reflect any new insights or reflections. For example, you could now say, "I'm afraid of speaking my truth, because the last time I did, I was deeply upset by the angry response I received."

Here are some examples of phrases that you could use to deal with the emotional issues underpinning a lack of assertiveness:

- "Even though I'm afraid to speak up, because I remember what happened the last time I spoke up, I choose to believe that I'm brave enough to speak up for myself now."
- "Even though he treats me rudely when I speak up, I choose to value myself by speaking my truth."
- "Even though I'm afraid they won't like me if I speak up, I deeply and profoundly love and accept myself."
- "Even though I'm afraid of being up here in front of all these people, I deeply and completely accept myself."
- "Even though I could never say what I wanted—my parents controlled what I could say … I was terrified to speak to them … I was expected to keep quiet—I deeply and completely love and accept myself."
- "Even though they won't understand my decision, I choose to accept my beliefs and stand by my decisions, and I completely love and accept myself."

EFT Tapping is a powerful yet non-invasive therapy that is simple and painless to use. Anyone can learn to do it. And you can practise it on yourself whenever you want, wherever you are, and on whatever issue you choose. It's not expensive or time-consuming, and you can use it on any emotional issue that interferes with the quality of your life. There are many books on the market that deal with the subject. There are also many practitioners out there who can help you with EFT.

Vibrational Healing

Vibrational healing is another approach that can be very effective in clearing blockages in the throat chakra and dealing with the fear that prevents a person from speaking his or her truth. Vibrational healing is nothing new. It has been practised successfully in numerous forms all over the world for thousands of years. But only recently has it come to the forefront in Western society. That's because scientists have finally developed instruments that are sophisticated enough to measure how and why this mode of healing works. Considered quackery in the past, many of these alternative techniques are now used in tandem with mainstream medical treatment.

Vibrational healing influences the body's energy field by changing its frequency. This involves consciously bringing higher vibrational frequencies into the body by using vibratory tools such as light, colour, sound, crystals, and aromatherapy. As the new energy frequencies are introduced or transferred into the physical and energetic bodies, the vibrations that have become unbalanced are adjusted to a positive state. Practitioners believe we experience illness or disease as a result of blockages or imbalances in the physical body itself or in the etheric body. These blockages slow down the vibration of the entire system. Therefore, if the vibration can be adjusted, good health and harmony can be restored.

Here are five natural vibrational remedies that can help you to clear any internal blocks you may have in connection with speaking your truth. As you'll see, most of these remedies are inexpensive and easy to get hold of, and you can start using them on yourself straight away. And if you want to go deeper, you can also find a local qualified practitioner in your area to help you.

Crystals

Crystals have been used in healing for centuries because of their vibrational energy properties. The Mayans, American Indians, and various Latin American and Indian cultures all have histories rich with stone healing. It is a matter of debate whether jewellery was originally invented for adornment or healing.

The Power of Speaking Your Truth

Crystals form in the earth's crust over millions of years at high pressure and in intense heat. Each one holds its own unique energy imprint. Placing a crystal on your body or within your electromagnetic field, raises your vibrational level as the crystal refracts and reflects light into your etheric field. This process filters stagnant energy out of your energy field and introduces into it the specific energetic properties of that crystal. Different crystals have different energies and properties, and between them they can affect the physical, emotional, mental, and spiritual aspects of a person.

Crystals can be carried or worn on your person, or they can be placed in a location where their healing vibrations can be felt by whomever is in the vicinity. Each type of stone has its own unique properties and benefits. Their colour, shape, and texture are all significant in determining their use. There are many crystals that can help with communication, and you can buy them in a size that's small enough to wear around your neck or carry in your pocket.

The throat chakra is blue in colour, so any crystal that's blue will help. Examples include azurite, turquoise, sodalite, aquamarine, blue topaz, blue tourmaline, blue obsidian, blue lace agate, and lapis lazuli. Each stone embodies a unique and specific kind of healing energy. Here are three of the most popular ones that can help you to speak your truth.

- Aquamarine helps to overcome the fear of speaking and is an excellent stone for teachers and presenters of all kinds. It relaxes the speaker into a state of consciousness in which he or she is fully aware of his or her own truths, wisdom, and feelings, and can articulate them with clarity and conviction. It's also an aid in difficult situations because it supports expression without anger.

- Blue lace agate helps to improve communication and self-expression because it heals the throat, gently dissolving any blocks to speaking truthfully.
- Turquoise is believed to enhance communication between the physical and spiritual worlds. When placed on the throat chakra, it releases old vows, inhibitions, and prohibitions, and allows the soul to express itself once again.

Owing to their energetic nature, crystals have to be cleansed regularly. There are various ways to do this. One of the most common is to submerge them in salt water (seawater is excellent) for a couple of days and then run them under the tap to clean off the salt. Another method is to bury the crystals in the garden for a few days, where the energy of the earth can cleanse and recharge them. After all, this is where they come from in the first place! Or you can place them in water and leave them outside overnight to bask in the moonlight.

You can easily buy crystals online and in shops that specialize in holistic health and complementary therapy–related products. It's often best to try to go to a physical store where you can see and touch the crystals and find the one that resonates with you the most.

Colour

Another complementary therapy that can be traced back to the distant past—this time to the ancient cultures of Egypt, China, and India—is colour therapy. Since colour is simply light of varying wavelengths, each colour has its own wavelength and energy frequency. All the colours in a rainbow are thought to carry their own unique healing properties.

The energy relating to each of the seven spectrum colours of red, orange, yellow, green, blue, indigo, and violet resonates with the energy of each of the seven main chakras, or energy centres of the body. Imagine the chakras as a set of cogs and the body as a clock,

The Power of Speaking Your Truth

and you will see how each cog needs to move smoothly for the clock to work properly. For good health and well-being, a balance of all the chakra energies is needed. When a certain chakra is imbalanced or blocked, colour therapy can help to rebalance or stimulate the energies by applying the appropriate colour to the body. The table below shows the feelings or experiences each colour promotes.[14]

Colour	Experience or Feeling
Red	Feelings of vitality, power, self-confidence, and safety
Orange	Feelings of sociability, happiness, increased social confidence, and joy
Yellow	Feelings of cheerfulness, mental clarity, confidence, and creativity
Green	Feelings of peace, love, harmony, and relaxation
Aqua	Feelings of purity, relaxation, and calmness
Blue	Feelings of improved communication and confidence in speaking
Indigo	Feelings of serenity, stillness, internal peace, and heightened creativity
Violet	Feelings of creativity, inspiration, selflessness, and generosity
Magenta	Feelings of emotional balance and internal relaxation
Pink	Feelings of relaxation, reduced aggression, and appetite suppression

We're focusing on clearing the throat chakra here, so the colour we're particularly interested in is blue. The colour blue has a direct healing and balancing effect on this chakra. Because the eyes and skin absorb colour, surrounding yourself in blue enhances your ability to clear any blocks to speaking your truth. You can wear blue

---

[14] https://www.mylighttherapy.com/colour-therapy.html.

clothes, drape a blue scarf around your neck, or even paint the room where you spend the most time a shade of blue you like.

It's interesting to note any strong colour preferences you have, because we're naturally and unconsciously drawn to colours that our mind, body, and soul need for perfect health and well-being. I used to offer a chakra-reading service and was constantly amused to find that people turned up to see me dressed in the exact same colour as the chakra that was out of balance. I remember one lady who had a thyroid problem. As I suspected, her throat chakra was blocked, and when I asked her what colour she was most drawn to she said, "Blue." This was no surprise to me, given that she'd shown up in a blue car, was wearing blue denim jeans with a sky-blue shirt, and was carrying a beautiful blue leather bag. When I pointed out that she instinctively knew what she needed to balance her thyroid gland and throat chakra, she laughed and said she'd recently redecorated her bedroom and it was now blue!

Colour therapy is holistic, completely safe, and non-invasive. You're surrounded by colour everywhere you go, so it's a really easy way to clear energetic blocks that keep you from living the life you want to live.

Sound and Music

People have used sound and music for thousands of years as powerful transformative tools for healing, shifting energy blocks, and bringing peace and balance to the mind, emotions, body, and soul. Himalayan singing bowls (a type of bell that vibrates and produces a rich, deep tone when played), for example, have been used in prayer and meditation throughout Asia for millennia and are now used to promote relaxation and well-being.

Sound therapists believe that we are all made up of different energy frequencies. They use sound frequencies to interact with our personal energy frequencies, with the aim of rebalancing the body's energy.

You can use sound healing to help energize and balance your throat chakra. This involves the therapeutic application of specific sound frequencies to the body and mind with the intention of bringing them into a state of harmony and health. One such set of healing frequencies is the Solfeggio frequencies. Solfeggio frequencies make up the ancient six-tone scale used in sacred music, including the beautiful and well-known Gregorian chant. The Benedictine monk Guido d'Arezzo (c. AD 991 —c. AD 1050) is thought to have developed the original Solfeggio scale, which was used by singers to learn chants and songs more easily. Today we know the Solfeggio scale as seven ascending notes assigned to the syllables "do" "re" "mi" "fa" "so" "la" and "ti".

Each note on the Solfeggio scale is thought to have specific healing properties. The one that aids expression and communication resonates at a frequency of 741 hertz. There are several recordings on the market that weave this specific healing frequency into beautiful pieces of music and guided meditations. They've been designed to help you release deep-rooted blockages and negative patterns of behaviour associated with a lack of assertiveness. Listening to these recordings can support you in expressing yourself freely, communicating effectively, clearing creative blocks, and feeling more determined and focused. It can also help with weight-control issues and a sluggish metabolism; hearing, throat, and thyroid problems; and even colds. An internet search will bring up some beautifully soothing pieces of music, and all you need to do is sit back, relax, and allow the music to wash over you. A particularly good one is "Purify Your Soul" by Glenn Harrold and Ali Calderwood, which can be purchased from online retailers. Over time it can help to clear, balance, and open up your throat chakra.

Flower Essences

Flower essences are another supportive tool for personal transformation and inner change. They are herbal infusions or decoctions made from the flowering part of a plant that capture the energetic imprints of the life force of that plant. When ingested, the energetic vibration interacts with the human energy field and evokes specific mental and emotional qualities.

A British physician, Dr Edward Bach, formulated the first flower remedies in the 1930s. He created thirty-eight essences to adjust emotional and mental imbalances. There are now several different flower remedy brands available in addition to those created by Dr Bach.

Flower essences work on the premise that the roots of all illness lie in negative emotions. The various essences work by enhancing positive states of mind and positive emotions, thereby dissolving their negative counterparts. Each flower represents a particular quality, and the essence works by transferring the energy of that quality to you. Essences are also believed to release blocks. They come in the form of drops that you simply place on your tongue or dissolve in water and sip.

When it comes to speaking your truth, flower essences that can help you include the following:

- lettuce, which soothes you when you're overstimulated so you can speak calmly, decisively, and authentically
- harebell, which gives you the confidence to speak up in groups and helps to attune you to your real needs
- malachite, which opens your heart so you can speak lovingly and compassionately
- blue sapphire, which inspires and uplifts you to speak your truth clearly and with courage

- viper's bugloss, which encourages you to speak with gentleness, care, and creativity, and to release judgement and criticism
- Bengal trumpet vine, which helps you to bravely share your soul truth and supports you with public speaking

Flower essences are readily available from complementary health stores. You can also order them online. You may want to pick one of the ones listed above and try it out. Or, alternatively, you can find a local qualified flower essence practitioner who can advise you on the best remedy for your specific issue. He or she can even blend essences together to create a tailor-made remedy especially for you.

Aromatherapy

Aromatherapy essential oils are a vibrational therapy that uses plant aromatics for the holistic healing of the body, emotions, mind, and soul. Essential oils, which are concentrated aromatic plant extracts collected through the process of steam distillation, have been used for thousands of years to invoke a range of positive qualities using the sense of smell.

Although the emotions that smells and fragrances evoke are highly personal, there appears to be a correlation between the scents of certain essential oils and the moods they create. The mood that a particular smell creates is largely down to the limbic system, which is the most primitive system in the brain. Therefore, by using certain essential oils, you can evoke feelings and emotional states that are particularly conducive to behaving more assertively. You may, for example, be looking for more confidence or courage.

Essential oils known for balancing the throat chakra and helping with assertiveness include basil, cedar, frankincense, and ylang-ylang. For greater confidence, you can use cypress, fennel, ginger, grapefruit, jasmine, orange, and pine.

The most common ways to use essential oils are inhalation, vaporization, massage, bathing, and applying drops to a compress. One of the easiest ways to enjoy the benefits of aromatherapy is to burn your chosen oil in a vaporiser and let the vapour fill the room you're in. If you wish, you can consult a qualified aromatherapist, who can advise you on which oils to use and how to use them for maximum benefit.

While the therapies and remedies suggested in this chapter will not, in and of themselves, automatically enable you to start speaking your truth, used in conjunction with the strategies outlined in the earlier chapters, they can significantly enhance your efforts. Clearing the energetic blocks that are held in your body and in your energy field will make it easier for you to express yourself fully and confidently.

Over the years, I have used many of the alternative therapies included in this chapter to clear my own energy blocks. For example, I love the colour blue and made a point of decorating my bedroom in a blue-and-purple colour scheme. That way I knew I was being visually exposed to the healing energies of this colour every day. I have a small bowl of blue crystals next to my bed that work on my energy field throughout the night. And I often fall asleep to the beautifully relaxing sounds of the Solfeggio frequencies that are woven into many of the guided meditations that I love listening to. Another activity I've found particularly helpful on my own personal journey from passivity to assertiveness is therapeutic writing. I love to write, and over the years I have used journaling to access, identify, and work through many of the hidden fears that previously stood in my way when it came to speaking up for myself. Most of the therapies included in this chapter are simple and easy to use. Why not give some of them a go?

Chapter 10

Assertiveness in Action

It's now time for us to revisit each of the five characters that have accompanied us on this learning journey and find out how they've learnt to speak their truth in their close relationships, their friendships, and their work environments. In the same way that you've been learning about the concepts and tools outlined in this book, so too have Zara, Jay, Sharon, Jasmine, and Aaron. We've already seen how they fared with some of the exercises outlined in the earlier chapters. Let's now recap their circumstances and the issues they've been struggling with and see how they've progressed on their self-development journeys.

Zara

Of all our fictional characters, Zara is the one who's had the most difficulty with speaking her truth. We've seen how, as a young housewife and mother, Zara struggled to communicate effectively with her husband. He worked long hours and often returned home late in the evening, and this upset Zara to the point that she began to harbour deep anger and resentment. This anger lay at the bottom of her passive-aggressive behaviour towards him, which manifested mainly as verbal shutdown and a distant attitude. Zara lived in a constant state of tension, and this adversely affected not only her own health (she developed hypothyroidism, hypertension, and muscular aches and pains) but also her five-year-old son, who started wetting the bed.

Zara began her personal development journey by engaging in the journaling exercise outlined in chapter 5. One evening after she'd put her son to bed, she sat down with a pen and paper and started writing about how upset she felt with her husband. She identified the specific issue: she wanted her husband to come home from work earlier so they could spend time together as a family. Following the prompts in the exercise, she asked herself, *What would happen if I asked him to come home early? ... And then what would happen? ... And then what would happen?* She continued to write down her thoughts exactly as they presented themselves in her mind, without censoring anything.

It took some time, but through this continual self-enquiry she eventually realized that she was frightened of being rejected by her husband. When she thought about disclosing her true feelings to him, she found that upsetting memories of her childhood surfaced. She recalled the awful bullying she'd experienced at school. Any time she drew attention to herself in class, she'd become an easy target for the class bully, who'd make her life miserable for the rest of the day. No one in her class ever came to her assistance, and she was left in a perpetual state of fear, feeling rejected, isolated, and vulnerable.

It came as a surprise to Zara that her present-day unhappiness was linked to her past in this way. She'd never questioned her feelings before and so had never made the connection. The process of reflecting on her fears and beliefs led her to a new insight: the reason she was scared to speak up and ask her husband to spend more time with her and their son was because he might dismiss, reject, or ridicule her. She soon realized that her silence wasn't merely a way of expressing her anger; it was also, up to this point, an unconscious self-protection mechanism.

Zara spent some time reflecting on her upbringing. She thought about the way her mother used to behave when she became angry or upset, and how she now dealt with such feelings herself. She recognized that her inability to speak up and process her anger came from the fact that her primary caregivers had never shown her how to do so. Whenever her mother was angry or upset, instead of articulating her thoughts and feelings and communicating with those around her, she would habitually shut down and refuse to say what was bothering her. Zara had simply learnt to model her mother's behaviour.

A further revelation for Zara came in the acknowledgment that her husband did not, and could not, automatically know what she was thinking and how she was feeling. A great deal of the tension between them arose from Zara's misguided belief about this issue. When she really thought about it, she understood for the first time that she couldn't possibly know what he was thinking unless he told her, so how could she expect him to know what was going on in her mind? Although she still felt very angry with him, she recognized that she needed to clearly state what was troubling her; otherwise, he would never know.

Despite all these internal breakthroughs, Zara still found it difficult to communicate with her husband. She sometimes struggled to say anything at all. Her fear was overwhelming, and it was clear that it was holding her back. She felt it would be easier for her if, at first, she simply focused on understanding herself better. She knew she needed to explore her fears in more depth and get in touch with her real feelings.

Zara had initially journaled as an isolated exercise, but it proved so insightful that she decided to keep a regular journal. Every evening after putting her son to bed, she wrote down what had happened during the day and, more importantly, her thoughts and feelings about what had happened. This was tough at first, but in time her writing became more emotion oriented. The more she wrote, the easier she found it to tune into her feelings and put them down on paper. It took a while, but she slowly began to connect with her anger in a way she'd never done before, and she was able to use writing as a tool to express it.

Because her hypothyroidism was a real concern for Zara, she decided to explore the connection between her condition and a possible block in her throat chakra. She continued to take her medication but began to explore several complementary approaches as well. She hadn't heard about the chakras before reading this book and was sceptical at first, but she thought she had little to lose by trying some of the holistic strategies suggested here. She'd always loved the colour blue and had many items of blue clothing, so she resolved to wear them as often as she could. She bought herself a set of blue pyjamas and began burning essential oils in her living room during the day; she particularly liked the smell of cedar. She also loved to wear jewellery, so she bought herself a turquoise crystal necklace, which she wore around the house every day.

Over the course of a few months of regular journaling, Zara noticed a change in her mood and emotional state. She felt less angry and less upset. She felt lighter and less tense. She felt that she had more insight into her situation and a greater understanding not only of herself but of her husband too, and this softened her attitude towards him. But she was still apprehensive about asking her husband to spend more time at home in the evenings. Before she tried to talk to him, Zara decided she needed to have a go at behaving assertively in a situation that felt less intense than the one with him. Since she was close to her mother and felt comfortable with her, it seemed a good idea to practise with her first.

An opportunity arose when Zara's mother phoned her to ask if she would come over to help her clear out her wardrobe. Zara thought about it for a moment and then concluded that it wasn't an essential or urgent task. So, for the first time ever, she prioritized her own needs (she wanted to go shopping instead) and said, "I can't come over today, but I promise I'll make some time later in the week." To her surprise, her mother was perfectly content to wait. This little success gave Zara the confidence she needed to have the conversation with her husband.

It took some courage, because she felt very uncertain of the outcome, but one evening she said, "Are you able to come home earlier in the evenings? It's very isolating being on my own every day, and it would be nice if you could spend a little more time at home with us." Her husband looked surprised and responded by saying that he stayed late at the office only because he thought she didn't like having him around! He said he'd love to spend more time at home. He couldn't come home early every day, because of his work commitments, but he would certainly try on some days.

By speaking up and articulating her needs, Zara overcame a major hurdle—one that had adversely affected her relationship with her husband. Because he responded positively, she gained the courage and encouragement she needed to continue her journey from passivity to assertiveness. Each time she took the risk of asking for what she needed, she found that she felt a little less afraid.

Jay

Now let's find out how Jay's personal development journey has progressed. Jay is the twenty-eight-year-old accounts assistant who works for a small company and lives on his own, having recently moved out of the family home. Jay's inability to speak his truth manifested at work at the time of his annual performance meeting with his manager. The fact that he hadn't received a pay rise since starting at the company angered and upset Jay. He believed he had worked hard and consistently met his targets, so he struggled to understand why this was the case, especially since many of his colleagues had been given promotions and pay rises during that time. However, he was reluctant to discuss the matter with his manager.

We learnt in chapter 5 why Jay was so afraid to do this. And in chapter 7, we saw how Jay began to uncover his fears and unhealthy beliefs for himself through a process of self-enquiry. He unearthed his fear of losing his job, his fear of not being good enough, his fear of being "found out", his fear of rejection, his fear of being ignored, and his fear of having to take on extra responsibility. He also identified some unhealthy rigid and awfulizing beliefs, such as *I must not draw attention to myself, my manager is going to refuse my request, my manager will realize I'm not good at my job, I'll lose my job, I'll lose my apartment*, and *I'll be the butt of office gossip*.

Taking these beliefs in turn, Jay began the process of disputing each one. He asked himself if each belief made sense, was true, and was realistic. This method of enquiry helped him to realize that there were other ways of perceiving the beliefs he held, and he eventually managed to come up with a much healthier set of beliefs. Many of Jay's beliefs were deeply entrenched, though, and the process of overturning them took some perseverance. To reinforce the new beliefs in his mind, he had to make sure he was constantly reminded of them. He wrote them out on small pieces of card and put them in prominent places around his home where he could easily see them. As he focused on his new beliefs, he began to feel more positive about his situation. His altered perspective gave him a sense of personal power and safety, and he decided he would ask his manager if it would be possible to talk about his pay.

But Jay still felt anxious about bringing up the subject at his annual review meeting. He decided that he needed to do some preparatory work. He liked the idea of retraining his subconscious mind by affirming positive statements to himself. He looked up the use of affirmations online and was surprised to discover that many successful and famous people around the world had used them as a tool for instigating personal change. He chose to affirm "I am good at my job. I am intelligent and competent. I speak up for myself, and I deserve a pay rise" twenty times, three times a day, for four weeks during the lead-up to the meeting.

Jay also liked the idea of rehearsing how he would conduct himself in the meeting using the rational emotive imagery technique described in chapter 8. Every evening after dinner, he sat down, engaged in some deep breathing to relax his mind and body, and visualized walking into his manager's office confidently and calmly. He connected with his affirmation and allowed the feel-good emotions that arose from the statement "I am good at my job. I am intelligent and competent. I speak up for myself, and I deserve a pay rise" to come to the fore. He imagined feeling calm, confident, and secure in the knowledge that he was doing a good job. He reminded himself that he wouldn't still be at the company if this were not the case. And, most importantly, he visualized himself assertively asking his manager if he could have his pay reviewed.

Jay connected with as many details of this imaginary scenario as he could. He visualized every aspect of the meeting in a positive way, from what he'd be wearing and his body language to how his voice would sound. While doing the visualization, it occurred to him that he could draw to his manager's attention the ways in which he had positively contributed to the work of the team. For example, he wasn't sure if his manager knew that he'd been supporting a colleague with a project that she'd been working on for the past four months. He also thought he'd highlight the fact that he'd consistently met his targets for the past six years. This gave him a feeling of self-assurance.

Jay repeated this exercise every evening for the two weeks leading up to his review meeting, and it didn't take long for him to begin to feel more comfortable. His anxiety began to subside, and he knew he could speak up for himself when the time came. Jay understood that he had no control over what his manager would say, but he knew that whatever happened, he could handle it.

Even before the meeting took place, Jay began to feel better about himself. He felt better about his colleagues too. And because his interactions with them were coming from a more positive place, his relationships in the office began to improve. This boosted his confidence even further.

The day of the meeting arrived. Jay continued to silently repeat his affirmations to himself throughout the morning and was able to tolerate the mild discomfort he experienced before seeing his manager. But once he was in the review meeting, he said everything he'd rehearsed and was pleasantly surprised to hear that his manager agreed with him. His manager acknowledged that he'd made a positive contribution and said he'd be considered for a pay rise, subject to him taking on additional responsibility for training new recruits in the IT systems used in the accounts department as they joined the team. Jay was very happy to do this. He knew the IT systems better than anyone and concluded that this was a mini promotion.

Sharon

As with Zara, Sharon's passive behaviour had been deeply entrenched in her psyche as a result of her childhood experiences. Sharon is the forty-two-year-old charity worker who grew up with an alcoholic father and a mother who had mental health issues. In chapter 7, we used the REBT model to look at how Sharon responds to requests for her time and attention, and the emotions that such situations

The Power of Speaking Your Truth

evoke in her. The process unearthed many of the fears and unhealthy beliefs that Sharon had been holding.

The core issue for Sharon was her diminished sense of self. Owing to her chaotic childhood, she hadn't had an opportunity to build a strong and robust sense of herself, and consequently her self-worth was particularly low. This had been driving her persistent people-pleasing behaviour all her life, as well as her unwavering desire to put the needs of others above her own. Sharon simply did not believe that she was good enough or worthy enough to put herself first. She also grew up in a home where it was dangerous to draw attention to herself, so she learnt at a very early age that it was safer to be quiet and compliant.

Although the REBT process helped Sharon understand why she was so terrified of speaking up, before she could muster the courage to start expressing her true thoughts and feelings to others, she knew she had to address her relationship with herself. The adage that "no one will respect you unless you respect yourself" struck a deep chord with her. It took her some time, but she gradually came to terms with the idea that, ultimately, she was the only person who could decide how important she was in her world. For the first time in her life, she came across the concept of personal power. She had never thought about it before.

When she became aware of the idea, she was fascinated and wanted to find out more. A few online searches led her to several interesting articles and blogs on the subject. What she discovered was that she always had a certain amount of power, no matter the situation. Even if she had no power or influence over other people in her life, she always had the power to choose *her responses* to those people. Her inner world belonged to her and her alone. She had power over what she thought and how she felt. She was never utterly powerless. This was quite a revelation to her.

Sharon had recently become an avid reader of self-help books, and she now developed a keen interest in learning about the effect her childhood experiences may have had on her, the impact of trauma in shaping her personality, and the effect that low self-esteem has on a person's life. Over time she learnt a great deal about herself and her patterns of behaviour. Although this new-found knowledge helped her question her attitude and outlook on life, Sharon realized that some of her issues were so deeply entrenched that, despite being very motivated, she wouldn't be able to change them by herself. This realization prompted her to invest in herself and seek out a therapist who could help her work on strengthening her sense of self.

She began attending counselling sessions once a week. It wasn't long before her counsellor noticed how harshly and unkindly Sharon treated herself. The therapist helped her to pay attention to her self-talk. She asked Sharon to notice the little voice in her head and to note down word for word any phrases that appeared regularly. Sharon had never consciously focused on her inner thoughts in this way before, and it was a shocking revelation to her. She recorded the following statements to show her therapist:

- "I can't do that."
- "I'm not smart enough."
- "I can't say that."
- "They'll think I'm stupid."
- "Why am I so dumb?"
- "I'm such an idiot!"
- "I just need to keep my mouth shut."
- "I'm such a weirdo—ugly, fat, and stupid."
- "No one loves me."
- "I'm not good enough."

On reviewing these statements, Sharon realized that her worst enemy was living inside her own head! No one had ever spoken to her the way she'd been talking to herself!

The Power of Speaking Your Truth

With the help of her therapist, Sharon's attitude towards herself gently started to soften. She began to recognize how negatively her childhood had affected her. It was clear that she hadn't been validated as a child and as a result had not developed a robust self-image. Sharon's therapist encouraged her to recognize the positive qualities she possessed. Sharon came to see that she was a valuable member of the team at the charity she worked for. She'd contributed to the success of many projects. She did a great deal of good in the world. She was kind and sensitive. She genuinely cared about other people and was helpful and attentive to their needs. She was organized and conscientious. She worked hard and made a difference in whatever arena she applied herself to. She had never recognized any of this before, and these realizations had a very positive effect on her self-esteem.

Sharon's therapist also encouraged her to make more time for herself. Together they explored all the things she could do to introduce more high-quality "me time" into her life. Sharon remembered that at school she had loved art and decided to enrol on an evening course where she could learn about painting with watercolour.

Sharon continued to attend therapy every week, and as she related her story—past and present—she gradually began to reconnect with her personal power. She felt better about herself, lighter, and more inspired. She came to realize that she was just as important as the next person, and this shift in attitude helped her to speak up for herself.

In therapy, Sharon set herself small assertiveness goals. She started by returning a cardigan she'd purchased from a local department store that turned out to be damaged. In the past, the thought of doing something like this would have been too much for her, and she would have worried about being blamed for the damage or become anxious about being treated dismissively by the shop staff. But now, in therapy, she rehearsed what she was going to say many times over so that she felt comfortable. She also told herself that it didn't really matter if it didn't work out the way she wanted; the important thing was that she just ask. She knew that returning the cardigan was within her legal rights, and that made her feel more secure. Sharon chose to go to the store early one morning when she knew it would be very quiet. She felt a little overwhelmed before she started speaking, but the shop assistant was very understanding and more than happy to exchange the item.

Through talking and self-reflection, Sharon noticed that her passivity was at its highest whenever someone put her on the spot and asked her to do something. She could think of several recent examples. Just the other day, her manager had asked her to urgently type up a document that one of her colleagues should have prepared beforehand. One of her colleagues had asked her to run out to reception to collect some post that a client had dropped off—a task she could easily have done herself. And a work friend had requested that she organize the refreshments for an office party that twenty other people would be attending. Previously, without giving these requests a moment's thought, Sharon would automatically say yes. She realized that this was where she needed to focus her attention, so she began to observe the times people asked her to do something at work. This exercise soon revealed that her colleagues were so sure she would agree to whatever they asked her that virtually everyone asked her to do all the unplanned ad hoc administrative tasks that came up during the day. They rarely asked her fellow administrative officer, even though she had the same duties and responsibilities as Sharon!

Sharon took this issue to therapy and with her therapist came up with a phrase that she could use to buy herself some thinking time. From then on, whenever anybody asked her to do something extra, she would make a point of looking the person making the request directly in the eye and say, "I just a need a minute to check my work schedule before I say yes to that. I'll get back to you shortly." This new strategy surprised a few people in the office to begin with, but because she said it clearly, calmly, and assertively, people had little choice but to say, "Okay."

The more Sharon practised at work, the more her confidence grew. One day Natasha asked her to babysit again. By now Sharon had sufficiently developed her self-worth to resist the temptation to immediately say, "Yes, of course." Instead she said, "Can I check my diary and let you know?" Natasha was surprised by this response and looked a little annoyed. She reacted straight away, saying, "It's never been an issue before. I'm sure you can do it!" Sharon knew Natasha very well and was expecting this reaction. She took a deep breath and said, "Yes, I know, but this time I need to think about it. I'll let you know either way by lunchtime." There was nothing Natasha could do but wait for a response.

Jasmine

Jasmine's journey from passiveness to assertiveness was like Sharon's in that it involved two things: dismantling the messages she'd internalized as a child and re-establishing her relationship with herself. As you may recall, Jasmine is thirty-two years old and works part-time in the human resources department of her local town council. She is married, has two young children, and lives with her husband, her husband's parents, and his younger brother.

Jasmine's upbringing engendered within her a quiet, compliant stance towards everyone in her life, where the needs of others were of paramount importance. As a result, she had lost all contact with her authentic self and struggled not only to articulate her truth but also to recognize what her truth was in the first place.

Jasmine found the journaling exercise described in chapter 5 fascinating. At school she had particularly enjoyed studying English literature and art, and she found that she took effortlessly to expressing her thoughts and feelings through writing and drawing. She began to set aside half an hour every evening, after putting the children to bed, to write in her journal. She reviewed her day and naturally started to focus on and explore any difficult feelings that had come up for her. The process of reflecting and journaling helped her to connect with her thoughts, feelings, and wishes, as well as her desires for her life. It automatically reconnected her to herself. She'd never focused on her inner world like this before. She was surprised at how much there was going on inside her own mind and body. The more she expressed herself through words and pictures, the more intrigued she became by the raft of fear-based and irrational thoughts she uncovered.

It wasn't long before she realized it was her own thinking patterns that had trapped her in a life of duty and obligation. The reality was that, regardless of what other people thought, said, did, or expected, what she did was down to her. It was her choice. She alone decided what to do, and when and how to do it. It became apparent to Jasmine that even though there were other people's expectations to contend with, the decisions she made had little to do with anyone else. When she thought about it, she realized she had taken on the role she played in the family of her own accord. No one had ever actually asked or demanded that she do any of the things she did on a regular basis. She'd just assumed that the other family members expected her to perform certain tasks. By taking responsibility, she had given them all a clear signal that she was happy to do the things she now resented. They'd simply left her to it and over the years become accustomed to her taking on a larger share of the domestic chores.

At first this realization upset Jasmine. She felt angry with herself. She felt foolish because she hadn't recognized what had been happening. But then it occurred to her that this was a positive thing—if she'd created this situation through her own behaviour she also had the power to change it. She could now work at changing her inner world and thus changing her outer reality as well. The truth was that this was an internal matter that had little to do with anyone else, because she alone was in control of her thoughts, beliefs, and attitudes.

As Jasmine began to dispute her unhealthy and irrational beliefs, she began to feel lighter and freer. She fully understood the need to maintain a healthy balance of power between her needs and other people's needs. She had no intention of putting her own needs above anyone else's, or of causing any disruption or arguments within the family, but she knew that for too long the scales had been tipped too far the other way. She needed to focus on her own needs more than she had ever done before.

Jasmine's anxiety attacks caused her considerable distress, so she resolved to find out how she could alleviate her symptoms. After seeing her doctor and doing some research, she realized that the answer to her anxiety lay in active relaxation. She decided to enrol on a weekly yoga and meditation class. Her husband was very supportive when she talked it over with him. He disclosed that he was becoming increasingly concerned about her anxiety and was relieved to know that there was something she could do to help herself without resorting to medication. He happily agreed to look after the children while she was away at her class.

As Jasmine learnt to stretch her body, release tension, focus her mind, and pay attention to her breathing, she soon began to feel calmer and more in control of her emotions and stress levels. She learnt to visualize herself sitting in a tranquil, scenic place, breathing in peace and stillness—a practice she continued at home. She discovered that playing calm, gentle music in the car helped her to relax and unwind too. The class gave her a change of scene and a break from home and work, where she spent most of her time; this in itself was psychologically refreshing.

Jasmine's endless duties and responsibilities around the house created the most pressure for her, and this was the area of her life she most wanted to change. But she knew that before she could summon up the courage to talk to the other members of her family, she had to work on her own self-esteem. She was able to talk to her husband, but whenever she thought about saying anything to her parents-in-law, she became anxious. It was clear that this was the issue she needed to work on.

The fear of criticism, disapproval, and rejection, which had come to light when she did the journaling exercise in chapter 5, loomed large in Jasmine's mind. With a view to disputing these fears, she now took each one in turn and wrote about it in as much detail as she could. By doing this, she was seeking to gain a better understanding of the power that her fears had over her. Next she went on to dispute each fear by asking herself if it was realistic and helpful to her on her journey towards assertiveness.

Most of the time, Jasmine found that her fears were not grounded in reality and were in fact a hindrance rather than a help. For example, she'd uncovered an unhealthy belief about being rejected and abandoned by everyone in her life. When she reflected on this belief, she soon realized that her husband would not leave her, and neither would her children. There was a possibility that her parents might be disappointed in her, but they wouldn't disown her. And she knew that her parents-in-law adored her children and that they could not expel her from the family without losing their grandchildren in the process. As Jasmine reflected and journaled, she began to convert her unhealthy beliefs into healthier ones—ones that allowed her to have flexible preferences as opposed to inflexible preferences that were non-awfulizing, that gave her the ability to tolerate a certain degree of frustration, and that focused on self-acceptance and self-respect.

For a long time, Jasmine had held the belief that she had to be the one to do all the household chores. Now she converted this into a more flexible belief, where she understood that while she was capable of doing all the chores, so were other members of the family. The old Jasmine was good at catastrophising. She'd convinced herself that

The Power of Speaking Your Truth

if she said even a word about reducing her duties, the entire family would disown her and she would end up losing everything. She now realized that was a little far-fetched. People might be upset and disappointed, but they wouldn't reject her in the way she'd initially believed. Jasmine realized she was experiencing a low frustration tolerance by presuming that she wouldn't be able to cope with any discomfort, and that she would end up having a mental breakdown.

Reflecting on who she was as a person, and the sheer amount of discipline, organizational ability, and inner strength she had to have to live her life the way she'd been living it up to this point, Jasmine realized that she was well able to cope with some temporary discomfort. Even if people were upset with her, she could handle it, provided that the issue that was most important to her (her workload) was addressed and resolved. Taking time out from her busy schedule to reflect on her life and relationships helped Jasmine to see that she gave a lot of herself and that it was time she started to expect some recognition and respect for everything she did for other people.

Jasmine was fortunate enough to have the love, understanding, and support of her husband. She was able to confide in him, and although they didn't always see eye-to-eye on every issue, he acted as a sounding board for her thoughts, feelings, and ideas, and this helped her move forward with her inner journey. At her weekly yoga class, Jasmine also met a lady called Kiran. One evening Jasmine disclosed to the class that she suffered from anxiety. This prompted Kiran to share her positive experience of using Emotional Freedom Technique. She offered to show Jasmine how to do the tapping herself.

Jasmine and Kiran became good friends. They discovered that they'd had similar life experiences and could relate well to each other. They began to meet for lunch, and Jasmine would often discuss her desire to be more assertive with Kiran. Kiran had never had any difficulty with being assertive and would sometimes warm-heartedly mock Jasmine's unhealthy beliefs, with the intention of helping her to change her perspective.

Jasmine's personal development journey consistently highlighted her low self-worth. To work on this issue, Jasmine decided to start a new "feel-good journal". She bought herself a beautiful little purple notebook, which she chose with great care so that she felt good just looking at it. In it, she began to record three things. Firstly, if anyone complimented her on anything, she would write it down. Jasmine had a wonderful sense of style and would often receive compliments on the way she dressed and looked. She was also a very good cook, and her food attracted many positive comments. Her conscientious and polite nature made her a pleasant work colleague, and her co-workers often told her that she'd done a good job. People had always complimented her in the past, but she simply hadn't allowed herself to register their admiring remarks. Now that she was looking out for these comments so she could write them down, they instantly became more noticeable.

Secondly, Jasmine used her new journal every night to write down all the positive things she'd done for other people during that day. This included washing and dressing the children, making their breakfast, dropping them off to school, going the extra mile at work, and helping members of her team with difficult tasks. As her focus shifted to how giving she was and the difference her contribution made to the people around her, she began to perceive her tasks in a more positive light, with more appreciation and less resentment. As soon as she started recording what she did for others, her emphasis moved away from feeling used and towards finding ways in which she could serve, purely because she wanted something positive to write in her journal. She began to feel good about herself. Her fear of rejection gradually diminished because it became clear how much she contributed to those around her. She knew it certainly wouldn't be in their interests to cast her out of the family!

The Power of Speaking Your Truth

Thirdly, Jasmine began to record five things that she was grateful for every day. She looked for five new things each time, and as with the previous practice, it forced her to actively notice all the positive things in her life. This little journal became a major source of feel-good energy for Jasmine. As it began to fill up with compliments and her own positive observations, she began to feel uplifted and more confident about herself and her place in the world. She began to feel important. She began to value herself more than she had ever done before.

In time, Jasmine noticed that she felt calmer and less burdened, with a new sense of personal freedom. She felt more in control of her life. Her anxiety dissipated, and she felt happier and more relaxed than she had done in a long time. Her family noticed this change in her, and because she felt more confident, she naturally started to share more of her inner thoughts and feelings with them. One afternoon, she felt that the time was right to talk to her mother-in-law about her workload within the home. She knew this would be the quietest time of day, with the other family members being out of the house and her mother-in-law relaxing with a magazine in the living room. Although Jasmine felt more self-assured and had visualized having this conversation many times prior to this moment, it was still a daunting prospect for her. In order that she would feel supported, she asked her husband to join them.

Jasmine sat down by her mother-in-law and said, "Mum, I'd like to talk to you about everything I do around the house. I find it hard to balance all the cooking and housework I have to do with looking after the children and going out to work. I'd like some more help." She spoke gently and kindly, but with firmness. Her mother-in-law reacted with surprise. Jasmine felt that she looked concerned, and maybe even a little anxious. As Jasmine explained how tiring and burdensome it was for her to manage all her domestic duties alongside her other responsibilities, her mother-in-law realized just how much it had been affecting her well-being. She confessed she had no idea Jasmine had been feeling this way. She spent a few minutes lamenting her own inability to help due to her various ailments and frailty, and then she said she was concerned about how they would manage to run the household if nobody took responsibility. After a few more minutes reminiscing aloud about how much she used to do when she was Jasmine's age, she concluded the conversation with "I can see you need some help, but I can't do as much as I used to. So what can we do?"

Jasmine and her husband had already thought about this. He told his mother he was willing to do more around the house at the weekends. And he added that they would ask his brother, who lived with them, to help with clearing up after meals and also with some of the cleaning. Seeing that she wouldn't have to pick up the slack if Jasmine did less, her mother-in-law felt happier and said she would do more to help prepare the family meals every day. Jasmine was content. Ideally, she had wanted to hire a cleaner, but she thought it would have been a step too far to ask for this. The proposed arrangement wasn't the perfect solution, but it was a good start, and she knew she had taken an important step forward by speaking up so she could bring more balance into her life.

As time went on, Jasmine became more willing to express her needs. Her cheerful and relaxed demeanour meant that when she did want to do something different from time to time, she simply had to ask and those around her would step in to accommodate her needs. Always mindful of other people's needs, Jasmine was careful not to demand things; she spoke politely and treated everyone with respect, and so any requests she made were rarely met with disapproval, which is what she'd been so afraid of in the past. Jasmine found that she had remained stuck in passiveness for so long not because of the people around her, as she'd initially suspected, but because of her own fears.

Aaron

Finally, it's time to see how Aaron has got on. Aaron is the thirty-seven-year-old IT consultant who has been married for fifteen years and has three young children. His desire to become more assertive arose from his increasing frustration and discontent with the way things were in his life, particularly at home with his wife. Because of her controlling behaviour, Aaron had become increasingly upset and resentful towards her. She disliked certain members of his family and became irritated with him if he ever expressed a wish to see his siblings—especially his brother. Aaron found his wife's nagging behaviour intolerable but struggled to make himself heard. He felt angry with her, but he also felt angry with himself. Deep down, he knew that he'd allowed this situation to persist by not standing up for himself, and that was why he'd become more and more powerless. What bothered him the most was not seeing his family.

Aaron had been feeling this way for months when he met up with an old school friend of his, Ethan, whom he hadn't seen in a long time. In the past, Ethan had also been friends with Aaron's brother, and as they were catching up, Ethan asked after him. Having to tell Ethan that he had no idea how his brother was embarrassed and upset Aaron deeply. Spending time with Ethan reminded Aaron of the "good old days" before he was married, when he and his brother would hang out with their friends. As they talked and enjoyed a few drinks together, Aaron began to feel more relaxed and less inhibited. The alcohol intensified his feelings after a while, and they became so overwhelming that he found himself telling Ethan about his predicament.

Ethan had a lot to say on the matter and helped Aaron to realize that there was a serious power imbalance in his marriage that he needed to remedy. Ethan emphasized the fact that Aaron worked hard and supported his family well. That alone entitled him to have more say at home. He also pointed out that a marriage is meant to be a partnership; but from what Aaron had disclosed, it sounded as though his wife was more of a dictator than a partner. Ethan said it wasn't right that she should come between him and his brother in the way she had, and he couldn't see how things could continue as they were. If they did, Aaron's marriage would be on the line. Deep down, Aaron knew that Ethan was right and that things had to change. He went home that evening feeling more strongly than ever before that he had to do something.

But before he could talk to his wife, Aaron knew he needed to understand his own thoughts, fears, and feelings. He knew from experience that if he raised the matter without any forethought, she would respond in her usual aggressive way and he would be shut down before he'd had time to properly explain how he felt. During the evening that Aaron spent with his friend, Ethan confided in Aaron as well and mentioned that he'd worked with a life coach who'd helped him to deal with a serious bout of anxiety. He'd been working too hard without realizing it, and the coach had helped him to make some changes and find a better work–life balance. Aaron reflected on whether he, too, needed some support to deal with his home situation, and a few days later he contacted Ethan to ask if his coach might be willing to work with him. Ethan was happy to pass on the coach's details, and Aaron arranged an appointment to see him.

Aaron was apprehensive at first, but after the first few sessions he realized that talking through his thoughts and feelings with an independent person in a confidential setting was helping him to work out what was really going on in his relationship with his wife. The sessions allowed him to address some of his unhealthy, unrealistic, and unhelpful thought patterns, as the coach gently challenged him. The coach also brought to his attention issues around personal boundaries, power dynamics, communication styles, self-worth, and, most importantly for Aaron, the internal obstacles that were keeping him stuck in his passive stance. With help from the coach, Aaron worked on his anger so that when he did raise the issue with his wife he would be able to do so from a calm, poised place rather than an emotionally charged one.

After several coaching sessions, Aaron's confidence began to increase. He began to feel more empowered. His coach helped him to practise acting assertively in imaginary interactions with his wife, and together they rehearsed how he was going to address the issues in his marriage. Aaron learnt that he had more power than he had initially realized, and he came to understand that if his wife loved and valued him, she would listen to his thoughts and opinions, provided he communicated them effectively.

After some dedicated work on himself, the day came when Aaron felt able to discuss how he felt with his wife. He chose a suitable time when the children were happily occupied and his wife wasn't too busy. He asked her if she'd like a cup of tea and said that he wanted her to sit down so he could talk to her. She declined the cup of tea but sat down. Aaron said, "I've been feeling really down for quite a while now. I feel that my thoughts and opinions don't count for anything in our marriage. It's only on rare occasions that I feel you hear me or value me. I need things to change." He went on to explain that he was happy for her to make most of the decisions in their life, but he could no longer tolerate being told what he could and couldn't do. He calmly told her how he felt she never listened to him or consulted him about anything. And he also revealed that he'd been so upset and challenged by the current state of the power dynamics between them that he'd paid to see a coach.

Aaron's wife was visibly taken aback on hearing that he'd been seeing a life coach without her knowledge and that he hadn't been able to speak to her directly. At first she responded in her usual aggressive way, demanding to know why he hadn't told her he was so unhappy. Aaron remembered the rational emotive imagery he'd rehearsed with his coach and did exactly as he'd envisaged. He remained calm and said, "Whenever I've tried to tell you, I've felt like you've shut me down. I don't feel heard." Once again, Aaron's wife became defensive and tried to explain that he was wrong, but he held his ground. His coach had advised him not to get into a row with his wife but to stay focused on asserting how he felt and what he desired for his own life. Arguing with her would simply make them fall back into their habitual way of relating to each other, and Aaron would once again have to back down.

As Aaron stayed calm and continued to assert himself, his wife slowly began to hear what he was saying. He explained that he had seen a life coach because he couldn't resolve the conflict that was going on inside him on his own. He valued his marriage and his family life; he loved his wife and wanted to be with her. But he was unhappy about how little his opinion mattered in their relationship. As they talked, it became clear to Aaron that his wife struggled to accept that it was her behaviour that was partially to blame for his unhappiness. She looked hurt and upset by what he was saying. She said she was shocked that he was this unhappy. She had presumed that everything was okay because he'd always backed down when they'd had a disagreement or she'd wanted to do things differently to him. But she also made it clear that she wanted to make things work between them. Aaron was pleased to hear that she didn't want their marriage to fail either, and that she didn't want him to be so unhappy.

Aaron said the life coach had suggested that couples counselling would be a good idea if they struggled to communicate effectively, but his wife felt they could work things out by themselves. She conceded that she needed to be a bit more mindful of Aaron's thoughts and feelings. Aaron had already realized he needed to speak up more and take more responsibility for his own life. He needed to connect with his own thoughts and feelings and then communicate them clearly to his wife. It took a while, but gently, over time, they started to listen to each other more intently and to talk things over when there were decisions to be made. As Aaron gained the space he needed to express himself, and as his wife sought to listen for his

The Power of Speaking Your Truth

needs and wishes, Aaron began to feel more empowered to speak his truth. He got better at telling his wife whenever he felt he wasn't being listened to, and this prevented her from falling back into her old ways. Gradually, they both learnt to listen to each other, be more open and honest about how they were feeling, and negotiate and compromise on the issues that were important to either one of them.

It took Aaron some time, but one day he finally brought up the issue of her resentment and controlling behaviour around his family. Aaron spoke openly about how much it upset him when he couldn't see his siblings. He told her that he missed their presence in his life and that this was the issue that caused him the most distress. His wife listened intently, but as was her habit, at first she tried to justify the situation by pointing out that he'd hardly ever mentioned the issue before. How was she to know he felt so upset if he hadn't said so all this time? Aaron remembered the work he'd done with his coach and chose to focus on asserting his feelings and expressing his preferences calmly and politely. After some discussion, they both realized that they had to compromise. Aaron learnt to accept the fact that his wife's feelings were so deep-seated that she couldn't bring herself to socialize with his family. His wife came to understand that, whatever her feelings may be, it was unjust and damaging to their relationship for her to insist that Aaron could not meet his family whenever he wanted to. She told Aaron that in future she would not stand in his way.

By finding his voice, Aaron had managed to address the power imbalance in his marriage. He was more than happy for his wife to make most of the decisions about their family life, because he trusted and valued the choices she made, but when it came to the things that really mattered to him, he began to speak up and stand his ground. He reconnected with his family and was slowly able to rebuild the relationships that he'd unwillingly neglected. Aaron would have felt more comfortable had his wife been able to extend a welcoming hand to his family too, but as she was not able to do so, he had to respect her decision. They eventually arrived at a place where they both agreed to disagree on the matter. The important thing, however, was that Aaron could now spend time with his siblings, and this made him feel much happier and more empowered.

As you've seen from the journeys that our fictional characters have made, speaking your truth is not always easy and straightforward. It takes time, commitment, and dedicated focus. It demands great self-awareness, courage, and a willingness to compromise. But the effort required is worth it. As you've seen with Aaron, Jasmine, Jay, Sharon, and Zara, the rewards include a healthier relationship with the self, improved self-esteem, clearer communication, less tension and conflict, and healthier relationship dynamics. Ultimately, the journey from passiveness to assertiveness results in an improved quality of life and a deeper sense of empowerment.

11
Chapter

Your Assertiveness Action Plan

In this book, we've explored what speaking your truth means in reality, as opposed to the common misconceptions that many people have. We've looked at why speaking your truth is an important life skill, the consequences of not speaking your truth, and the positive outcomes you can expect when you do find the courage to communicate openly and honestly. We've picked our way through the fears and unhealthy beliefs that are keeping you trapped in your passive behaviour, and we've worked through the REBT model, which can help you to develop a new way of relating to yourself and others. We've also explored a range of alternative therapies that can gently support you as you embark upon your journey towards assertiveness.

Changing Long-Standing Habits

It's highly likely that if you've struggled to speak your truth and be assertive in the past, it has now become your habitual way of relating to others. When we form a habit, it becomes our default position simply because we've always done things that way; we know what we're doing, and we feel safe. We're all naturally drawn towards our habitual ways of relating because they feel comfortable. For this reason, habits can feel ingrained and difficult to overcome. But if you persevere, you will find that you can break through your habits and establish a new mode of behaviour—one that is healthy and more beneficial for your well-being. If you find the courage to experiment, commit to the process of personal development and change, can tolerate the initial discomfort of stepping outside of your comfort zone, and are willing to seek help from others if necessary, you will soon establish a new habit; and this habit will eventually become your new default position.

We all go through a period of uncertainty, confusion, and even discomfort when we first start to learn a new skill. If you're a driver, cast your mind back to your first few driving lessons. Do you remember being anxious? Do you remember feeling unsure about what to do? Do you remember feeling slightly overwhelmed by all the things you had to take in, remember, and do? You certainly weren't alone if you felt that way.

Whenever we learn a new skill, we go through four distinct stages: unconscious incompetence, conscious incompetence, conscious competence, and unconscious competence. We all start off in stage one. This is where we are unconsciously incompetent. Now, as far as being assertive is concerned, this is the point at which you don't even know what speaking your truth is. You're completely unaware that you don't know, and therefore you don't care. You have no desire to learn about it, because you're unconscious of the fact that you need to change in any way.

The fact that you're reading this book shows that at some point you moved into the second stage—conscious incompetence. Somewhere along the way, you arrived at the realization that you need to move to a different place within yourself and relate to others differently; you became consciously aware that you do not know how to speak your truth. Perhaps it was a single incident that triggered this insight, or perhaps as time went on, you became dissatisfied with your life. Somehow you realized you need to learn a new skill, and you became consciously aware of your incompetence. You then chose to read this book.

Now, armed with the knowledge you've gained from this book, and by using the suggested self-help tools, you're aiming to move to stage three: a place of conscious competence. As you apply the ideas we've discussed here to your life, you will slowly move to the point where, knowing you must do something different, you start to make a conscious and consistent effort to take a different approach. This stage requires focus, commitment, and effort. It's likely to be the most uncomfortable stage. Going back to the analogy of learning to drive a car, this is the stage at which a new driver must consciously remember to check the gearbox, put on his or her seat belt, turn the ignition, check the mirrors, indicate, and move the pedals in order to move the car.

When you've practised enough times, you will eventually move to stage four—a place of unconscious competence. This is the end goal. This is when you know how to speak your truth so well that you don't even have to think about it. It becomes who you are—your natural default position. At this stage, you become comfortable with and competent at speaking your truth. It becomes effortless.

I hope this book has provided you with the tools to move from a place of conscious incompetence to the edge of conscious competence. To comfortably move into conscious competence, and finally unconscious competence, you will have to do several things.

What's Best for You

First and foremost, you will have to resolve deep in your heart that speaking your truth is in your own best interests and that all the effort you'll have to make will eventually pay off because you'll feel more positive about yourself, your place in the world, your relationships and the quality of your life. You can reread chapters 3 and 4 to remind yourself of the probable consequences of not moving to a more assertive place and the benefits of doing so. This is an essential step, because without it any efforts you make will lack conviction. For some people, this will be easy to do, while others will have to continually strengthen their resolve.

It's Going to Be Uncomfortable

Secondly, you will have to accept—and indeed expect—that some feelings of discomfort, and even fear, will arise in the short term. These feelings are completely natural. As we've already discussed, they arise whenever we do or learn something new. Everyone experiences fear to varying degrees when he or she steps outside of his or her comfort zone. I'm pretty sure you've already experienced similar feelings in the past. Do you recall your first day at school, the first time you travelled on public transport on your own, the day you started your first job, or the first time you left home and started fending for yourself? If you're a parent, do you remember the fear and anxiety that accompanied the early stages of parenthood? These are common experiences that most of us can relate to. We all experience some level of uncertainty, confusion and fear when we do something for the first time. The chances are that if you've lived through any of these situations, you know you can handle and work through the similar feelings that will come up for you when you first start speaking your truth.

In the initial stages, expect an increase in some uncomfortable feelings, expect your negative self-talk to increase, and expect your old unhealthy thoughts, beliefs, and habits to pull you back into your old ways. But whatever happens, *you must not give in*. These are all perfectly natural responses to change, and you will have to persist until they subside. You can rest assured that they will do so.

The Resistance

Thirdly, expect resistance from those around you, as well as yourself. It's highly likely that you will experience some level of opposition from your family, friends, and colleagues. Just as you're used to behaving in a certain way, the people in your life will be accustomed to seeing you behave in that way too. In this book, we've focused primarily on the inner work you need to do to facilitate your move from passivity to assertiveness. But you may find that another barrier to speaking your truth comes from those closest to you. If, over the years, you have given away your power to family and friends, then they will have a personal stake in keeping you as you are. Your submissiveness and accommodating attitude will suit them because their needs and desires are more likely to be fulfilled that way.

When you start speaking up for yourself, you may find that people get upset with you or disapprove of you. Expect this, tolerate the uncomfortable feelings that will inevitably come up for you, and hold fast to your commitment to change. You will have to persist with this for a while to reclaim your power.

Should you find yourself on the receiving end of other people's disapproval or outright criticism, you will have to harden your resolve both emotionally and intellectually. Remind yourself constantly *why* you set out to be more assertive in the first place. Remind yourself of the harmful consequences if you do not follow through. Remind yourself that speaking your truth is about equality; it's about finding the balance between your own needs and others' needs. As we discussed in chapter 1, assertiveness is not about always getting your own way. By learning to speak your truth, you're respecting others while at the same time respecting yourself.

It's likely that the unhealthy beliefs that have underpinned your passive behaviour will plague you in the initial stages of your transition from passivity to assertiveness. There will be a part of you that feels guilty about upsetting others. Remember that it is not your intention to hurt others and that you're not responsible for other people's feelings or their happiness. This same voice will tell you you're being selfish. Remember that this is not true. You're merely coming back into a place of balance after being in a state of imbalance for so long. It's helpful to think of a pendulum that has swung too far to one side and got stuck there. You're bringing it back into the middle, where it should have naturally been all along. If you apply the principle of equality, listen attentively and respectfully to other people's needs and wishes, and then arrive at a decision that prioritizes your own needs after taking all these factors into account, you are not being selfish; you are being assertive. After all, if you don't put your needs above other people's *in some cases*, then who will do that for you? If you are truly assertive, most of the time you will place your own needs *alongside* other people's needs, but you will also be willing to put yourself first when your well-being demands it.

Assertiveness is about showing respect, kindness, courtesy, and empathy to others and showing respect, kindness, courtesy, and empathy to yourself. It will pay to remember that so you're not put off by the initial disturbances you're likely to experience, both within yourself and from others. If you expect this inner and outer commotion, when it begins to feel uncomfortable you won't be surprised and thrown off balance so much that you retreat into your passive behaviour.

It will serve you to remember that you are liberating yourself from a way of communicating that has kept you enslaved for years.

No longer will you be a doormat who has no say in your own life. It's your life; you owe it to yourself to be true to who you are.

We all know that practice is the key to getting better at anything we want to master. The more you practise, the more confidence you will gain in yourself and your new skills. And the more confident you become, the easier it will be for you to continue being assertive, until one day you find that all the discomfort has disappeared.

Devising Your Personal Strategy

To start off your practice, it's a good idea to invest some time in devising a targeted strategy. You need to plan carefully, and you do this by starting small. Don't be tempted to charge into every situation you encounter and start speaking your mind! If you pick too big a challenge, there's a danger that you will fail, and this will undermine your confidence. For example, it's not advisable to pick the most cantankerous or most powerful person in your life to try out your new skills on. Remember: your aim is to practise and to gain confidence through that practice. You don't want to be knocked down at the outset, because if you are, there is a strong possibility you will never try again. If you end up backing down at your first attempt, it will be harder for you to do it the next time round. Therefore, it is critical that you initially pick a situation in which you have a reasonably high chance of success.

Take some time out to prepare your case on paper. By writing things down and carefully planning the interaction, you will clarify your thoughts, become more focused, and be less likely to go off on a tangent or feel overwhelmed.

Sit down and write out a list of bite-sized challenges that you face in your day-to-day life. You could start by making a list of all the people in your life and putting them in order from the easiest, gentlest, and least frightening person to the most difficult, antagonistic, and most frightening person. This will be a subjective exercise based solely on how you experience the various people in your life. At one end of the spectrum, there will be those who are easy to talk to. They are the people who make you feel emotionally safe—the ones who listen to you, hear what you have to say, and accept you with a loving, kind attitude. At the other end of the spectrum, there will be people you try your best to avoid because they intimidate you and make you feel anxious. They are the ones you have to pluck up courage to talk to, and when you do talk to them, you try to keep the conversation light and superficial for fear of inviting drama and confrontation. They are the ones who frighten you. Once you've made your list, select the person at the top (the gentlest one) and try out your assertiveness skills on that person first. See how you get on. As you gain confidence, you can then work your way through the list.

The next step is to list situations that challenge you and order them in terms of perceived difficulty, from the least challenging to the most challenging. You may already be aware of situations in your life that require more assertiveness on your part. Or you may want to identify situations that are likely to arise in the future in which, judging by your past behaviour, you know you're likely to behave passively and go along with other people's suggestions regardless of your own preferences. Think about those areas of your life in which you would like to see some change, and resolve to act differently. And so you set yourself up for success and not failure, pick something easy to begin with.

Generally speaking, it's easiest to start speaking your truth to people you don't know. Service industries, such as shops, restaurants, insurance companies, and utility companies, are a good place to start. People who work in this sector are inclined to listen to you because you're the customer and their job is to ensure you remain a satisfied one. They're trained to keep you happy. So as long as you're being reasonable, you shouldn't experience very much resistance. You're likely to find that your voice is heard.

The Power of Speaking Your Truth

Again, generally speaking, the most difficult people to tackle at the beginning are family members—especially close ones. It's best to wait to confront them until you've gained some confidence through practice. Your family will be accustomed to your quiet and compliant behaviour, and they will have the most to lose if you find your voice and begin to step into your power. When you begin to assert your needs and opinions to family members, you may find that they react with fear or that there is a temporary negative backlash. Should this happen, you must remind yourself persistently that speaking your truth is not about winning or losing. It's not about getting your own way all the time, and it's certainly not about shouting, arguing, or using your voice to abuse others. After all, you're aiming to make your life better, not worse!

Only you can fully understand the relationship dynamics in your life, so the important thing to remember is that only you can decide when to stand your ground and when to give in. If someone does react badly, check that you've listened carefully to that person's concerns and behaved respectfully towards him or her, but also try to remember that that person is choosing his or her own reactions and that you're not responsible for his or her anger or upset.

By being gently and respectfully persistent about the things that are important to you, you will slowly start to reshape the existing relationship dynamics in your life. If you modify your relationship dynamics with care, tact, and sensitivity at a slow enough pace, you might be pleasantly surprised to find that your family doesn't even notice that there has been a change. You may not even face any resistance.

Here is an example of a list of challenges in which an assertive approach is required, placed in order of difficulty, starting with the least difficult:

- returning a faulty item to a shop
- sending back a meal at a restaurant because it's cold or you don't like it

- asking the friendly neighbour's children to stop kicking a ball into and damaging your garden hedge or fence
- being assertive with your sister about the need to take equal responsibility for visiting your elderly parent
- being assertive with your manager when you feel he or she hasn't distributed work fairly across the team
- being honest with your spouse about how you want to spend your leisure time
- letting your mother-in-law know how she makes you feel when she refuses to hear your point of view

Once you've made your list, pick the first situation you've written down. Then reflect on the following points. Write down your answers so you are clear about what you need to do to tackle the situation.

1. Identify the emotion that is most likely to stop you from being assertive in this situation. It will be fear in some form. When you expect to feel the emotion in advance, it will not creep up on you unawares so you become overwhelmed and shy away from pursuing your goal.

   For example, "I'm anxious about talking to the sales assistant in case she refuses my request or starts to argue with me."

2. Identify what you don't like or agree with and therefore need to challenge.

   For example, "These shoes aren't comfortable, which is why I need to return them."

3. Decide what outcome you'd like.

   For example, "I'd like a full refund."

4. Plan how you will compromise if the outcome you want isn't possible.

   For example, "If I can't have a full refund, then I will settle for a credit note."

5. Decide what you're going to say.

   For example, "I will say, 'Hi, I bought these shoes last week, but they feel really uncomfortable, so I'd like to return them, please.'"

6. Choose the best time to have the conversation.

   For example, "It's quieter during the week and earlier in the day, so I'll go to the shop on Tuesday morning before work."

Go back over what you learnt in chapter 1 about good assertiveness skills. When it comes time to have the conversation, be mindful of your body language. Relax your shoulders, approach the person you want to talk to confidently, keep your head up, make good eye contact, smile, and speak with a resonant voice.

Always remember that being assertive is a two-way process. You need to actively listen to what the other person is saying and respond accordingly. If you're returning an item to a shop, as in the above example, it's quite likely that the sales assistant will ask to see your purchase receipt and inspect the item before giving you a full refund. In more challenging situations, you will have to listen carefully to the responses you're getting, consider each one, decide how you feel about it, and then respond accordingly. To listen effectively, you will need to keep calm. Taking long, deep breaths can really help with this.

With the most challenging situations, it's a good idea to go over the learning from chapters 7 and 8. You will need to invest time and energy in working through the REBT model, step by step. To recap, you will need to become aware of your emotional response to the situation, identify the activating event, uncover the unhealthy beliefs you're holding, dispute those beliefs, arrive at a new understanding, find new healthier beliefs that create positive feelings, use affirmations and rational emotive imagery to internalize your new beliefs, and finally change your behaviour so you act in a more assertive manner.

It will serve you to remind yourself often that you won't always get your way. You're not going into battle, and you don't need to "win" every time you speak up for yourself. You simply have to pluck up the courage to state your truth, focus on listening to the other person, and then arrive at a compromise. Sometimes you will get what you want, because in that situation your wishes and needs take priority, and sometimes the other person will get what he or she wants, because at that point his or her needs and wishes are more important. You're striving for equality, not supremacy. When you start changing your behaviour, there's a danger that the pendulum might just swing too far the other way—from passiveness to aggressiveness. This is something you need to be mindful of.

Occasionally you will come across someone who will strongly resist your efforts to speak your truth and will continually deflect your attempts at assertion by avoidance or counter-attack. In these situations, you must apply another strategy—that of focus and repetition. Plan out your interaction as outlined earlier so you're completely clear about what you want to say. Then, if you find that the other person isn't listening to you, just focus on your script and keep repeating the same statement over and over again. Continue to make your case succinctly and clearly and don't get sidetracked. Keep to the point. That way you won't become overwhelmed or confused by having too much information in your head. Eventually the other person will have to either listen or walk away. But you will have remained in your power. And you will have spoken your truth.

You will have to practise. You will have to persist. You will have to believe in yourself. There will be some discomfort along the way. You may experience mild, or even strong, opposition from people who have a vested interest in keeping you as you are. But know that the effort you're making to be more assertive will serve you well for the rest of your life.

Your new way of relating to others will liberate you from the shackles of your own mind and your upbringing. It will allow you to step wholly into your personal power. It will increase your self-worth and your self-esteem. It will enable you to set healthy boundaries by showing people that they must acknowledge you and treat you with respect. And, ultimately, it will lead you to a more peaceful and fulfilling life in which your needs are valued in equal measure to the needs of the people around you.

Finally, remember that *you* are in control. You decide which situations you're going to speak up in. You decide the pace at which you want to go. And you decide which relationships demand a change in dynamics.

It's going to feel scary at the beginning, but if you can dig deep, find a little courage, and tolerate some temporary discomfort, one day you will look back and find that this was a small price to pay for getting back your personal power—and your life.

Good luck! You can do it.

About the Author

Harinder Ghatora is a holistic life coach and counsellor. She runs a private practice in West London in the UK and offers a range of services that are designed to help people live a healthy and balanced life. Harinder works with all aspects of a person's being: the mind, body, emotions, and spirit. She supports her clients in overcoming personal challenges and becoming more self-empowered.

A graduate from the London School of Economics, Harinder forged a successful managerial career in local government, specializing in research and statistics, for eighteen years before retraining as a counsellor, NLP coach, and healer. Her time is now fully devoted to supporting others through one-to-one work, group work, workshops, and e-products.

For further information about Harinder's work, visit her website: www.harinderghatora.co.uk

CPSIA information can be obtained
at www.ICGtesting.com
Printed in the USA
FFHW022003100919
54878604-60588FF

9 781982 224653